Twic

THE TWILIGHT SAG/

ISBN 978-91-87309-00-7

Jengel Förlag AB
Samuel Permans gata 9, 831 31 Östersund,
tel 063-10 54 10, www.jengel.se

This book is an extended, updated and translated version of the Swedish book
"I populärkulturturismens spår Twilight+Vacation=Twication©"

Text: Christine Lundberg, Maria Lexhagen, Sigrid Mattsson
English translation: Clare Barnes, Åre Translation
Cover photo: Diego Mancuso
Graphic design: Lena Ljungkvist (www.lenagrafiskform.se)
Print: Tallinna Raamatutrükikoja OÜ, 2012

Twication™

THE TWILIGHT SAGA TRAVEL EXPERIENCE

Christine Lundberg   Maria Lexhagen   Sigrid Mattsson

Etour

European Tourism Research Institute, ETOUR, develops and communicates knowledge about tourism and travel. That by having an ongoing dialogue and interaction with the travel and tourism industry. ETOUR was established in 1997 and belongs to the Tourism Department at Mid Sweden University.

www.miun.se/etour

Mid Sweden University

Mid Sweden University with its three campuses in Härnösand, Sundsvall and Östersund counts about 20 000 students and more than 1 000 employees. The University is Sweden's youngest and a place where people can meet, be inspired and think in new ways. Unique study programmes and research with high scientific quality has made Mid Sweden University a resource for development and growth.

www.miun.se

Contents

Acknowledgements

We would like to thank stakeholders of Twilight tourism in Forks, La Push and Port Angeles, WA, US – Forks Chamber of Commerce, Forks Visitor Center, Forks Outfitters, Twilight Tours in Forks, Team Forks, Lapelles, the Mayor of Forks, Miller Tree Inn aka "Cullen House", the Quileute tribe and Bella Italia. In Vancouver, Canada we would like to express our appreciation to Tourism Vancouver, Tourism Vancouver Visitor Center, British Columbia Film Commission and On Location Tours. We would also like to thank the following stakeholders in Italy; the Mayor of Volterra, Consorzio Turistico di Volterra, representatives from the local municipality in Montepulciano and ProLoco Montepulciano. A special thank you to press officer Diego Mancuso in Montepulciano, who so graciously allowed us to use one of his photos from the New Moon film set for our book cover. Thank you!

In addition to this, we wish to extend our thanks to the more than 1,600 participants in our Twilight tourism web survey and to the following social media networks that have helped us distribute the link to it, such as TwilightSweden.se, Spunk-Ransom.com, Thinkingofrob.com, RobertPattinson.no, BellaandEdward.com, TwilightLexicon.com, Twilightish.com. Your help has been invaluable for our research!

A big thank you to our fellow Twilight Saga researchers who have contributed to our research: Associate Professor Mia Larson, Lund University, Sweden, Stavroula Wallström, University of Borås, Sweden and Dr Kristina Lindström, Gothenburg University, Sweden. We would also like to extend a thank you to our publisher Jengel Förlag AB and staff for an effortless collaboration! Thank you!

Twilight characters

Isabella "Bella" Swan is the series' main character. At the start of the first book she is seventeen years old, and moves from her mother in Arizona to live with her father in the rainiest town in the USA – Forks, Washington. She starts high school there, and meets and falls in love with Edward Cullen, the school's most desirable boy – but he has a secret past. Bella Swan is played by the American actress Kristen Stewart.

Edward Cullen is a 107-year-old vampire at the start of the first book, though he has the body of a 17-year-old. He is a tortured soul with no real meaning in life until he meets Bella. Edward Cullen is played by the British actor Robert Pattinson.

Charlie Swan is Bella's father and is police chief of the little town of Forks, Washington. Charlie Swan is played by the American actor Billy Burke.

The Cullen family's figurehead is the vampire doctor Carlisle Cullen. Along with his wife, Esme, he has adopted the "children": Edward, Alice, Jasper, Rosalie and Emmett, all of whom are vampires. They regard themselves as vegetarians, as they only drink the blood of animals due to their respect for human life.

Jacob "Jake" Black has Native American ancestry and is Bella's best friend. He lives on the reservation in La Push and belongs to the Quileute tribe. He and the others in his tribe are also werewolves. Jacob Black is played by the American actor Taylor Lautner.

Quileute is a tribe that is located in La Push, just outside Forks, Washington. They are descendants of shape shifters and can transform into wolves/werewolves when necessary. The gene that drives this transformation is only activated in the presence of vampires.

The Volturi is one of the oldest vampire covens in the Twilight Saga. The coven's base is the town of Volterra, Italy. Their self-proclaimed task is to ensure that all vampires keep the secret of vampires' existence. They can be said to be the vampire world's only royalty and are generally feared by the vampire community.[1]

---

[1] http://www.twilightlexicon.com/the-lexicon/character-bios/

Introduction

More than a quarter of a million fans from around the world have travelled to the little town of Forks, population 3,532, in the north-western USA, to experience Stephenie Meyer's best-selling romantic book – and now film – series, *The Twilight Saga* (hereafter Twilight).[1] This comprises four books, which have now sold over 116 million copies globally[2], and five films. The first four films that have so far been released at the cinema and on DVD/BlueRay have earned over USD 3.1 billion.[3] The story is about Bella, who moves to her father, the police chief of the rainiest town in the USA. There, she meets the vampire Edward Cullen and his family, and falls in love with him. Her new best friend is the werewolf Jacob Black, but because vampires and werewolves are deadly enemies, according to legend, the scene is set for a real drama that has attracted visitors to this little town.

Twilight tourism in Forks, which is just one of a number of different "Twilight destinations" around the world, has

Twilight fan standing next to the welcome sign in Forks, WA, USA.

been described as a fantastic gift to the town. Marcia Bingham, manager of Forks Chamber of Commerce, says,

> "It's a phenomenal gift. I can't thank Stephenie enough. I can't imagine that she had any idea of how enormous this would grow and how big a following it would be".[4]

These types of destinations are usually described as *settings*[5] and comprise places that are associated with a story found in a book, film or TV series. These differ from *locations*[6], which are destinations where films or TV series were recorded. Famous examples of the latter are the *Lord of the Rings* films in New Zealand and *Braveheart* in Ireland. In the case of Twilight, the story is primarily played out in four different *settings* – Forks, La Push and Port Angeles in Washington, USA, and Volterra in Italy. All of these destinations now have considerable tourist flows due to the phenomenon that is the series; this is despite none of the films being recorded in these places. They were primarily recorded in Portland, Oregon, in the USA; British Columbia (e.g. Vancouver, Squamish, Tofino) in Canada; and Montepulciano in Italy. These *locations* have also had documented tourist flows during and after the recording of the films.[7]

These examples can be used to illustrate what has been described in the literature as *location dissonance,* i.e. the difference between where a story takes place and where it is filmed[8], but regardless of whether the place has figured in a book or on screen, it attracts tourism of varying degrees.[9]

Journeying to places that are associated with media for popular culture, such as books, TV series or films, is not in itself a new phenomenon. This has been demonstrated by Frost's[10] historical description of film tourism, in which he traces this form of tourism back to the first half of the twentieth century. However, although this form of tourism is not a new phenomenon, it has not been until the most recent decade that there has been increased interest in how it can participate in creating an attractive image for destinations and how it can influence tourist flows.[11] The fact that this form of tourism is based on both reality and fiction[12] and that it creates an emotional tie between the destination and the tourist, may perhaps explain why it is attracting an increasingly large and selective group of modern tourists who are searching for experiences. One explanation for this emotional link to a place that the potential tourist may never have previously visited is that a film, book or television production includes dramatic events that create an emotional association between the tourists and the characters or the places in which they are located.[13] In addition, this form of tourism has a significant storytelling element, which is an increasingly common and powerful tool in experiential production.[14]

This modern form of tourism is particularly interesting as it is very demand governed[15] and is part of creating future travel behaviours among tourists in general. In addition to being governed by demand, it often grows rapidly and surprises stakeholders at the receiving destinations; consequently, this can cause capacity problems for accommodation and other tourism services. This often rapid growth means that it is difficult to predict where and to what extent this type of tourism may occur. Film tourism is often a specific type of tourism that attracts broad target groups, i.e. not primarily certain age and/ or socio economic groups.[16]

Another factor that makes it difficult to predict this form of tourism is that books, films and TV series, for example, are not primarily created to generate tourism at new destinations. There is a link between these creative industries and tourism, but at present there are few partnerships and developed products. One of these, but perhaps the best known and largest scale example of cross-border activities in film production and tourism, is Walt Disney's Disneyland and now the Disneyworld Resorts in the USA and Europe. The background to the origins of Walt Disney's investments in tourism is said to be the desire for reduced impact on actual filming sites and the staff that working at them.[17] Instead, tourists were offered the chance to visit a themed pleasure park that is linked to the productions.

Finally, this form of tourism has been accused of having a short life length, often called sustainability in tourism literature. However, Frost's[18] history-based review of global film tourism destinations shows the long-term potential of this form of tourism. Several negative effects on destinations that are mentioned in the literature are poorly prepared destinations, the loss of control – primarily over which tourists are attracted and at what volume, increased prices, a limited capacity to manage increased tourism, negative environmental impact and differences in how the destination is experienced in comparison to the image conveyed by the film, which can lead to decreased customer satisfaction.[19]

References

[1] **Destination Forks**: The Real World of Twilight (2010) DVD, Summit Entertainment.

[2] **http://www.publishersweekly.com/pw/by-topic/childrens/childrens-book-news/article/44733-little-brown-to-publish-official-twilight-guide.html** [Retrieved: 17th of September 2012]

[3] **The-numbers.com** (2012). [Retrieved February 23rd, 2012 from http://www.the-numbers.com/movie/Twilight-Saga-Breaking-Dawn-Part-1-The] **The-numbers.com** (2012). [Retrieved February 23rd, 2012 from http://www.the-numbers.com/movies/2008/TWLIT.php] **The-numbers.com** (2012). [Retrieved February 23rd, 2012 from http://www.the-numbers.com/movies/2009/TWLI2.php] **The-numbers.com** (2012). [Retrieved February 23rd, 2012 from http://www.the-numbers.com/movies/2010/TWLI3.php] **The-numbers.com** (2012). [Retrieved February 23rd, 2012 from http://www.the-numbers.com/movie/Twilight-Saga-Breaking-Dawn-Part-1-The]

[4] **OPB News**: http://news.opb.org/article/vampire-tourism-provides-novel-twistforks-wa/ [Retrieved: 18th of April 2011]

[5] **Riley**, R., Baker, D. & Van Doren, C.S. (1998) Movie Induced Tourism. *Annals of Tourism Research, 25*(4), 919–935.

[6] **Tooke**, N. & Baker, M. (1996) Seeing is Believing: The Effect of Film on Visitor Numbers to Screened Locations. *Tourism Management, 17*(2), 87–94.

[7] **The Los Angeles Times**, 13th of December 2008. '*Twilight*' Brings Fresh Blood for Forks Tourism.[http://long island.newsday.com/twilight-brings-fresh-blood-to-forkstourism-1.888416. Retrieved: 27th of September 2011] **The Vancouver Sun**, 18th of April 2009. *Twilight Sisters Cross Continent to Grab Peek of Robert Pattinson in New Moon Shoot: What Makes Teen Vampire Romance Series So Compelling to Devotees of All Ages?* [http://www.vancouversun.com/entertainment/Adult+Twilight+fans+from+Nashville+Vancouver+search+Robert+Pattins on+Moon+gang/1503715/story.html. Retrieved: 27th of September 2011] **The Vancouver Sun**, 30th of March 2009. *New Moon Rumours Lure Twilight Fans to Possible Location Shoots Around Vancouver.* [http://www2.canada.com/vancouversun/news/sports/canucks/story.html?id=1444828. Retrieved: 27th of September 2011]

[8] **Frost**, W. (2006) *From Backlot to Runaway Production: Exploring Location and Authenticity in Film-Induced Tourism.* Working Paper Series ISSN 1327-5216 pre-

sented at the Second International Tourism and Media Conference in Melbourne, Monash University, Department of Management, Australia.

Tooke, N. & Baker, M. (1996) Seeing is Believing: The Effect of Film on Visitor Numbers to Screened Locations. *Tourism Management, 17*(2), 87–94.

Riley, R., Baker, D. & Van Doren, C.S. (1998) Movie Induced Tourism. *Annals of Tourism Research, 25*(4), 919–935.

[9] **Beeton**, S. (2005) *Film-Induced Tourism*. Channel View: Clevedon UK.

[10] **Frost**, W. (2006) *From Backlot to Runaway Production: Exploring Location and Authenticity in Film-Induced Tourism*. Working Paper Series ISSN 1327-5216 presented at the Second International Tourism and Media Conference in Melbourne, Monash University, Department of Management, Australia.

[11] **Hudson**, S. & Ritchie, B. (2006) Promoting Destinations via Film Tourism: An Empirical Identification of Supporting Marketing Initiatives. *Journal of Travel Research, 44*, 387–396.

Lee, S. Scott, D. & Kim, H. (2008) Celebrity Fan Involvement and Destination Perceptions. *Annals of Tourism Research, 35*, 809–832.

Riley, R., Baker, D. & Van Doren, C.S. (1998) Movie Induced Tourism. *Annals of Tourism Research, 25*(4), 919–935.

Connell, J. (2004) Toddlers, Tourism and Tobermory: Destination Marketing Issues and Television-Induced Tourism. *Tourism Management, 26*, 763–776.

[12] **Frost**, W. (2009) From Backlot to Runaway Production: Exploring Location and Authenticity in Film-Induced Tourism. *Tourism Review International, 13*(2), 85–92.

[13] **Kim**, H & Richardson, S. (2003) Motion Picture Impacts on Destination Images. *Annals of Tourism Research, 30*, 216–237.

[14] **Mossberg**, L. & Nissen Johansen, E. (2006) *Storytelling: marknadsföring i upplevelseindustrin*. Studentlitteratur AB: Lund.

[15] **Müller**, D. (2006) Unplanned Development of Literary Tourism in Two Municipalities in Rural Sweden, *Scandinavian Journal of Hospitality and Tourism, 6*(3), 214–228.

[16] **Hudson**, S. & Ritchie, J.R.B. (2006) Film Tourism and Destination Marketing: The Case of Captain Corelli's Mandolin. *Journal of Vacation Marketing, 12*(3), 256–268.

[17] **Frost**, W. (2006) *From Backlot to Runaway Production: Exploring Location and Authenticity in Film-Induced Tourism*. Working Paper Series ISSN 1327-5216 presented at the Second International Tourism and Media Conference in Melbourne, Monash University, Department of Management, Australia.

Marling, K.A. (1997) *Designing Disney's Theme Parks: The Architecture of Reassurance.* Flammarion: New York.

[18] **Frost**, W. (2006) *From Backlot to Runaway Production: Exploring Location and Authenticity in Film-Induced Tourism.* Working Paper Series ISSN 1327-5216 presented at the International Tourism and Media Conference in Melbourne, Monash University, Department of Management, Australia.

[19] **Beeton**, S. (2001) Smiling for the Camera: The Influence of Film Audiences on a Budget Tourism Destination, *Tourism Culture and Communication*, *3* (1), 15–25.
Beeton, S. (2005) *Film-Induced Tourism*. Channel View: Clevedon UK.
Riley, R., Baker, D. & Van Doren, C.S. (1998) Movie Induced Tourism. *Annals of Tourism Research, 25*(4), 919–935.
Tooke, N. & Baker, M. (1996) Seeing is Believing: The Effect of Film on Visitor Numbers to Screened Locations. *Tourism Management*, *17*(2), 87–94.

Tourism and popular culture

The art forms described above – film, television and literature – are usually categorised as belonging to the field of popular culture (hereafter pop culture). This area also includes radio, fashion and music, and is the cultural form consumed by the social majority.[1] Pop culture has been defined as culture that is appreciated by many people, and is also called mass culture.[2] This is often placed in opposition to "fine culture", where a line is drawn between art (fine culture) and entertainment (pop culture).[3] Another criterion for pop culture is that it is commercial: *"It is first when a type of expression is placed relative to a market on which financial considerations are made and where cultural products are produced and consumed, that we can talk of it as belonging to popular culture"*. In addition, this form of culture is described as easily accessible (not intellectually demanding) and linked to recreation and entertainment.[4]

Research into pop culture is often called *"studies of everyday life"* and has cultural studies such as sociology, ethnology, media studies, literary studies and anthropology as its starting point.[5] Central areas have been the concept of text, i.e. different cultural expressions as carriers of meaning (e.g. written texts, pictures, clothes) and how these are coded by a sender and decoded by a receiver. Lindgren believes that pop culture texts *"reflect and express many people's needs (aesthetic and otherwise), so the text says something about the audience"*.[6]

Studies with pop culture as a basis for tourism have destination and tourist/fan perspectives. When a destination perspective is used, concepts such as *commoditization*[7], *staged performance* and *authenticity*[8] are often studied; these deal with the extent to which a tourism experience is organised for visitors and to what degree it can be regarded as "genuine". Other studies that originate in pop culture demonstrate how celebrities' associations with places can influence tourists' perceptions of these destinations.[9]

The area within which the majority of research has been focused is that of film tourism. This is where, according to Beeton's[10] review, development has moved from confirming the phenomenon and calculating tourist flows[11], to focusing on more complex factors such as tourists' motivations[12] and the management of and impact on destinations.[13] Current research focuses on postmodern interpretations of concepts such as *authenticity, hyperrealism* and *simulacra,* which takes the discussion beyond simplified explanations of film as a marketer of places.[14] Baudrillard believed that hyperrealism means that the border between the simulated (the fictional in Twilight's case) and the real is dissolved and that simulacra are simulated codes (substitutes for reality) that are communicated via consumption and the media.[15]

Up until now a great deal of research has been case study based, which means that specific destinations and/or films/TV series have been examined. One of the most studied cases is *The Lord of the Rings* films' effects on tourist flows and tourism experiences in New Zealand. For example, the borders between authenticity and the simulated in this form of tourism have been studied.[16] Additionally, in this case, tourists' experiences of authenticity have been compared with experiences that can be attained through religious pilgrimages.[17] *The Lord of the Rings* phenomenon has also been studied on the basis of tourists' expectations and their experiences of guided tours in which printed material and the guide's storytelling abilities are vital factors.[18] These tourists' experiences have also been studied with a focus on the extent to which the degree of *hyperreality* influences satisfaction with the guided tour. The results showed that the representation of hyperreality in the tour experience increases satisfaction. For example, the tourist can be in the films' environments and recreate scenes from the films him/herself (= high level of hyperreality). The borders between fabricated authenticity and national authenticity and how they are connected have also been studied.[19] Furthermore, the significance of an image strategy has been highlighted in the case of *The Lord of the Rings*, where advantage has been taken of the phenomenon's impact on the image of the country and tourist flows.[20]

The relationship between national identity and the development of pop culture tourism has also been the focus of another well-studied case – *Dracula tourism* in Romania. This has included discussions of how the development of this form of tourism can be part of social development in a post-communist Romania.[21] The balancing act between using a somewhat unwelcome stereotype of Romania – *Dracula* – as an opportunity for national development (such as through tourism) has been investigated.[22] Studies of *Dracula tourists* in Transylvania have shown that visitors, through their imaginations, are part of the process of reshaping the myth of Transylvania as a place.[23] Furthermore, people's need to link fictional stories such as *Dracula* with real places by visiting them has been examined in a research study. The results show that this can be explained by two needs: one is making comparisons between the described and the real landscapes; the other is being located emotionally in this environment.[24] Another study of *Dracula tourism* in Bran Castle looks at visitors' collective creation of tourist experiences along with other tourism stakeholders.[25]

A region in which the tourism effects of a number of film and television series have been studied is the *British Isles*.[26] There is research that has looked both at specific films or television series, as well as studies that have investigated how the image of entire areas and tourism flows has changed due to films and television series. One example, with which many people are familiar, is the blue door in London's *Notting Hill* that was shown in the hit film of the same name (1999) and which featured the actors Julia Roberts and Hugh Grant.[27] An even more contemporary example that has created tourism comprises the books and films about the young wizard *Harry Potter* (1997–2011). One of these studies has noted a 100 per cent increase in tourism at Alnwick Castle, Northumberland, over 2001–2002 due to the book and film series.[28] *Harry Potter,* along with *Sherlock Holmes* and *Peter Rabbit,* has been identified as a highly significant factor in the creation of Great Britain's image among Japanese tourists.[29] The film *Braveheart* (1995), in which Mel Gibson plays the Scottish freedom fighter William Wallace, is perhaps one of the most important associations to link Scotland to pop culture. One of the studies that looked more closely at this phenomenon documented a 25 per cent increase in tourism to Stirling Castle over the years 1995–1997.[30]

Many British television series have generated tourist flows to various parts of the country, for example, the popular area of Yorkshire, and there have been studies of how the image of destinations is communicated through film and television series.[31] There are many places in Great Britain where television series have been a catalyst for tourism development, such as the *Heartbeat* series set in the North York Moors National Park.[32] The *Darcy effect* that grew out of the BBC production of *Pride and Prejudice* (1995) has also been examined and has confirmed the importance of films and series to the tourism industry.[33] On the Scottish *Isle of Mull* there have been studies of how the tourism generated by local television series influences local companies' profits.[34] Television series' impact on tourism has also been investigated in *South Korea*. Studies show that Korean television series and celebrities have an influence on tourists' positive associations with destinations, increasing their level of intention to visit places linked to these series.[35]

Australia is a country where there has been documented research into films' effects on the tourist industry; for example, studies have been made of how the actual production of a film can be regarded as long-term tourism on the Australian *Gold Coast*.[36] As with the Scottish folk hero William Wallace, films have been made about Australia's own legend, *Ned Kelly*, which have resulted in heritage tourism.[37] Additionally, the image of the Australian outback has been analysed in order to understand the image that tourists expect when they arrive at a destination.[38] In another part of the world, *South America*, the film *The Motorcycle Diaries* (2004) has reinforced the image of South America as a good value ecotourism destination[39] among young American students, as well as creating a desire among Canadians to travel to the countries shown in the film.[40]

Furthermore, the film *The Beach* (2000), about backpacker Richard's search for the perfect beach on his travels through Thailand, has been studied to discover how Internet travel companies have used the film to market their trips to Thailand.[41] Another film by the same director, Britain's Danny Boyle, *Slumdog Millionaire* (2008), has also been studied from the perspective of how *India* is depicted in the film.[42] Tourism to destinations associated with fictional action heroes such as *James Bond*[43] (1953–) and *Laura Croft: Tomb Raider*[44] (2001) has also been documented. Research has also been conducted around films in the drama genre that have created international tourism and increased tourist flows, such as *Captain Corelli's Mandolin*[45] (2001) on the island of *Cephalonia* in *Greece, The Sound of Music*[46] (1965) in *Salzburg* in *Austria*, as well as *Dances with Wolves* (1990) in *Kansas, USA* and *Thelma & Louise* (1991) in *Utah, USA*.[47]

From a customer's perspective, current research shows – as previously mentioned – that this type of tourism tends to create strong emotional ties to places that the visitor has found through film, literature or television productions, which can be expressed in many different ways. For example, they may constitute a primary reason to travel for some visitors, while for others the reason may be a visit to a theme park or a guided tour at a destination that they have found in a fictional context. One explanation for these emotional ties to a place that the potential tourist may never have previously visited, is that a film, book or television production includes dramatic events that create an emotional link between the tourist and the characters or the places in which they are located.[48] However, some people believe that visitors who have been attracted to a place via a film/television-related experience are not attracted by the real experience of the place, but by being able to be filled by the mythology created in the interaction between film and reality.[49] Beeton believes that motives to travel for film tourism are more complex than those allowed for by the push-pull model that is popular within tourism.

Visitors travel to film-related places to re-experience a happening or a feeling from a film, to strengthen a legend/myth, stories/fantasies, or for the status (celebrity) that a place may have.[50] From a destination perspective, in the case of Twilight this phenomenon has primarily brought new life to the small and declining timber town of Forks in Washington State, USA, but has also generated significant tourist flows in the Tuscan towns of Volterra and Montepulciano in Italy, as well as in Vancouver and British Columbia, Canada (see below for more information about these Twilight destinations). As regards Forks, the destination has embraced the development of tourism and is now almost entirely dependent on the production of tourism experiences. Visitors of all ages visit the town to experience the characters' everyday lives and even expect to meet a vampire or werewolf (characters) or two on the town's streets or in the surrounding forests.[51]

A Swedish example is the book, and now film, series the *Millennium Trilogy*. Since 2009, this has attracted 10,000 Swedish and international tourists to Stockholm, every year, to participate in guided Millennium walks. In this case, Stockholm is both a *setting* and a *location*. Forecasts for this tourism are that it is expected to generate an increase in commercial guest nights of 3.44 per cent (totalling 2,158,000), and an increased number of day visitors and private guest nights, with total forecast spending of SEK 430 million in Stockholm in the period 2009–2013.[52]

Even in early film research it was observed that it can be difficult to determine a film's popularity just by evaluating financial factors. Instead, the thought was that semiotics (messages and signs), ideology, and psychology are of great significance. Even if many studies since then have focused on measuring the importance of film tourism in terms of an increased number of visitors, increased awareness and knowledge of a destination should be regarded as indicators of success via film tourism.

Research into film tourism has progressed from a focus on the number and type of visitors to understanding the effects of tourism on the environment, society and economy, as well as an understanding of why people travel on the basis of film/television experiences, how marketing affects this and how an image is created. There is also more recent research with a more postmodern approach that focuses on identity, myth and imagination, and the research area has also become more multidisciplinary (e.g. media research, cultural research, sociology, anthropology, business studies).[53] There is a need for more research into film tourists' motivations and the business-related and financial aspects of film tourism – because a film tourism destination's success is currently probably due more to chance than to good planning and design – an understanding of the significance of the interest in a film, and what influences the life length of this form of tourism.[54]

References

[1] **Lindgren**, S. (2005) *Populärkultur: Teorier, metoder och analyser*. Liber: Malmö.

[2] **Strinati**, D. (2004) *An Introduction to Theories of Popular Culture*. Routledge: NY.

[3] **Heilbrun**, J. (1997) The Competition between High Culture and Popular Culture as Seen in the New York Times. *Journal of Cultural Economics, 21*, 29–40.

[4] **Lindgren**, S. (2005) *Populärkultur: Teorier, metoder och analyser*. Liber: Malmö, p. 33.

[5] **Lindgren**, S. (2005) *Populärkultur: Teorier, metoder och analyser*. Liber: Malmö. **Traube**, E.G. (1996) "The Popular" in American Culture. *Annual Review of Antropology, 25*, 127–151.

[6] **Lindgren**, S. (2005) *Populärkultur: Teorier, metoder och analyser*. Liber: Malmö, p. 15.

[7] **MacCannell**, D. (1973) Staged Authenticity: Arrangements of Social Space in Tourist Settings. *The American Journal of Sociology, 79*(3).

[8] **Cohen**, E. (1988) Authenticity and Commoditization in Tourism. *Annals of Tourism Research, 15*(3), 371–386.
Xie, P.F., Osumare, H. & Ibrahim, A. (2007) Gazing the Hood: Hip-Hop as Tourism Attraction. *Tourism Management, 28*, 452–460.

[9] **Lee**, S. Scott, D. & Kim, H. (2008) Celebrity Fan Involvement and Destination Perceptions. *Annals of Tourism Research, 35*, 809–832.

[10] **Beeton**, S. (2010) The Advance of Film Tourism. *Tourism and Hospitality Planning & Development, 7*(1), 1–6.

[11] **Riley**, R. & Van Doren, C. (1992) Movies as Tourism Promotion: A Push Factor in a Pull Location. *Tourism Management, 13*, 267–274.
Tooke, N. & Baker, M. (1996) Seeing is Believing: The Effect of Film on Visitor Numbers to Screened Locations. *Tourism Management, 17*(2), 87–94.
Riley, R., Baker, D. & Van Doren, C.S. (1998) Movie Induced Tourism. *Annals of Tourism Research, 25*(4), 919–935.

[12] **Beeton**, S. (2005) *Film-Induced Tourism*. Channel View: Clevedon UK.
Riley, R. & Van Doren, C. (1992) Movies as Tourism Promotion: A Push Factor in a Pull Location. *Tourism Management, 13*, 267–274.

[13] **Mordue**, T. (1999) Heartbeat Country: Conflicting Values, Coinciding Visions. *Environment and Planning, 31*, 629–646.
Mordue, T. (2001) Performing and Directing Resident/Tourist Cultures in Heartbeat Country. *Tourist Studies 1*(3), 233–252.

[14] **Beeton**, S. (2010) The Advance of Film Tourism. *Tourism and Hospitality Planning & Development*, *7*(1), 1–6.

[15] **Baudrillard**, J. (1988) Simulacra and Simulations. I *Selected Writings*, Poster, M. (Ed). Stanford: Stanford University Press, p. 166–184.

[16] **Tzannelli**, R. (2004) Constructing the 'Cinematic Tourist': The 'Sign Industry' of the Lord of the Rings. *Tourist Studies, 4*(1), 21–42.

[17] **Buchmann**, A., Moore, K. & Fisher, D. (2010) Experiencing Film Tourism: Authenticity & Fellowship. *Annals of Tourism Research, 37*(7), 229–248.

[18] **Buchmann**, A. (2010) Planning and Development of Film Tourism: Insights into the Experience of Lord of the Rings Film Guide. *Tourism and Hospitality Planning & Development, 7*(1), 77–84.

[19] **Jones**, D. & Smith, K. (2005) Middle-Earth Meets New Zealand: Authenticity and Location in the Making of The Lord of the Rings. *Journal of Management Studies, 42*(5), 923–945.

[20] **Croy**, W.G. (2010) Planning for Film Tourism: Active Destination Image Management. *Tourism and Hospitality Planning & Development, 7*(1), 21–30.

[21] **Tanasescu**, A. (2006) Tourism, Nationalism and Post-Communist Romania: The Life and Death of Dracula Park. *Journal of Tourism and Cultural Change, 4*(3), 159–178.

[22] **Light**, D. (2007) Dracula Tourism in Romania: Cultural Identity and the State. *Annals of Tourism Research, 34*(3), 746–765.
Shandley, R. Hamal, T. & Tanase, A. (2006) Location Shooting and the Filmic Destination: Transylvanian Myths and the Post-Colonial Tourism Enterprise. *Journal of Tourism and Cultural Change, 4*(3), 137–158.

[23] **Light**, D. (2009) Performing Transylvania: Tourism, Fantasy and Play in a Liminal Place. *Tourist Studies, 9*(3), 240–258.

[24] **Reijnders**, S. (2011) Stalking the Count: Dracula, Fandome and Tourism. *Annals of Tourism Research, 38*(1), 231–248.

[25] **Huebner**, A. (2011) Who Came First – Dracula or the Tourist? New Perspectives on Dracula Tourism at Bran Castle. *European Journal of Tourism Research, 4*(1), 55–65.

[26] **Bolan**, P. & Williams, L. (2008) The Role of Image in Service Promotion: Focusing on the Influence of Film on Consumer Choice Within Tourism. *International Journal of Consumer Studies, 32*(4), 382–390.
Brereton, P. (2006) Nature Tourism and Irish Films. *Irish Studies Review, 14*(4), 407–420.

Meaney, S. & Robb, J. (2006) Shooting Ireland: The American Tourism Market and Promotional Film. *Irish Geography, 39*(1), 129–142.

Young, A.F. & Young, R. (2008) Measuring the Effects of Film and Television on Tourism to Screen Locations: A Theoretical and Empirical Perspective. *Journal of Travel & Tourism Marketing*, 24(2), 195–212.

[27] **Busby**, G. & Klug, J. (2001) Movie-Induced Tourism: The Challenge of Measurement and Other Issues. *Journal of Vacation Marketing, 7*(4), 316–332.

[28] **Mintel** (2003) *Film Tourism – International* (October). Mintel International Group: London.

[29] **Iwashita**, C. (2006) Media Representations of the UK as a Destination for Japanese Tourist: Popular Culture and Tourism. *Tourists Studies, 6*(1), 59–77.

[30] **Scottish Enterprise Forth Valley** (2000) *The Importance of Tourism.* Briefing Note 5. Forth Valley Enterprise: Stirling.

[31] **O'Connor**, N., Flanagan, S. & Gilbert, D. (2010) The Use of Film in Re-Imagining a Tourism Destination: A Case Study of Yorkshire, UK. *Journal of Vacation Marketing, 16*(1), 61–74.

O' Connor, N., Flanagan, S. & Gilbert, D. (2008) The Integration of Film-Induced Tourism and Destination Branding in Yorkshire, UK. *International Journal of Tourism Research, 10*, 423–437.

[32] **Mordue**, T (2001) Performing and Directing Resident/Tourist Cultures in Heartbeat Country. *Tourism Studies, 1*(3), 233–252.

Tooke, N. & Baker, M. (1996) Seeing is Believing: The Effect of Film on Visitor Numbers to Screened Locations. *Tourism Management, 17*(2), 87–94.

[33] **Sargent**, A. (1998) The Darcy Effect: Regional Tourism and Costume Drama. *International Journal of Heritage Studies, 4*(3–4), 177–186.

[34] **Connell**, J. (2004) Toddlers, Tourism and Tobermory: Destination Marketing Issues and Television-Induced Tourism. *Tourism Management*, 26, 763–776.

Connell, J. (2005) 'What's the Story in Balamory?': The Impacts of a Children's TV Programme on a Small Tourism Enterprise on the Isle of Mull, Scotland. *Journal of Sustainable Tourism, 13*(3), 228–255.

[35] **Kim**, S., Long, P. & Robinson, M. (2009) Small Screen, Big Tourism: The Role of Popular Korean Television Dramas in South Korean Tourism. *Tourism Geographies, 11*(3), 308–333.

Kim, S. & O'Connor, N. (2011) A Cross-Cultural Study of Screen-Tourists' Profiles. *Worldwide Hospitality and Tourism Themes, 3*(2), 141–158.

Kim, S.S., Agrusa, J., Lee, H. & Chon, K. (2007) Effects of Korean Television Dramas on the Flow of Japanese Tourists. *Tourism Management, 28*(5), 1340–1353.

Lee, S. Scott, D. & Kim, H. (2008). Celebrity Fan Involvement and Destination Perceptions. *Annals of Tourism Research, 35*, 809–832.

Lin, Y-S. & Huang, J-Y. (2008) Analyzing the Use of TV Miniseries for Korea Tourism Marketing. *Journal of Travel & Tourism Marketing, 24*(2–3), 223–227.

[36] **Ward**, S. & O'Reagan, T. (2009) The Film Producer as the Long-Stay Business Tourist: Rethinking Film and Tourism from a Gold Coast Perspective. *Tourism Geographies, 11*(2), 214–232.

[37] **Frost**, W. (2006) Braveheart-ed Ned Kelly: Historic Films, Heritage Tourism and Destination Image. *Tourism Management, 27*(2), 247–254.

Beeton, S. (2004) Rural Tourism in Australia – Has the Gaze Altered? Tracking Rural Images through Film and Tourism Promotion. *International Journal of Tourism Research, 6*(3), 125–135.

[38] **Frost**, W. (2010) Life Changing Experiences: Film and Tourists in the Australian Outback. *Annals of Tourism Research, 37*(3), 707–726.

[39] **Shani**, A., Wang, Y., Hudson, S. & Gil, S.M. (2009) Impacts of Historical Film on the Destination Image of South America. *Journal of Vacation Marketing, 15*(3), 229–242.

[40] **Hudson**, S., Wang, Y. & Gil, S.M. (2011) The Influence of a Film on Destination Image and the Desire to Travel: A Cross-Cultural Comparison. *International Journal of Tourism Research, 13*, 177–190.

[41] **Tzannelli**, R. (2006) Reel Western Fantasies: Portrait of a Tourist Imagination in The Beach (2000). *Mobilities, 1*(1), 121–142.

Law, L., Bunnell, T. & Ong, C-E. (2007) The Beach, The Gaze and Film Tourism. *Tourist Studies, 7*(2), 141–164.

[42] **Mendes**, A.C. (2010) Showcasing India Unshinding Film Tourism in Danny Boyle´s Slumdog Millionaire. *Third Text, 24*(4), 471–479.

[43] **Reijnders**, S. (2010) On the Trail of 007: Media Pilgrimages into the World of James Bond. *Area, 42*(3), 369–377.

[44] **Winter**, T. (2002) Angkor Meets Tomb Raider: Setting the Scene. *International Journal of Heritage Studies, 8*(4), 323–336.

[45] **Hudson**, S. & Ritchie, J.R.B. (2006) Film Tourism and Destination Marketing: The Case of Captain Corelli's Mandolin. *Journal of Vacation Marketing, 12*(3), 256–268.

[46] **Im,** H.H. & Chon, K. (2008) An Exploratory Study of Movie-Induced Tourism: A Case of the Movie The Sound of Music and Its Locations in Salzburg, Austria. *Journal of Travel & Tourism Marketing, 24*(2–3), 229–238.

[47] **Riley**, R. & Van Doren, C. (1992) Movies as Tourism Promotion: A Push Factor in a Pull Location. *Tourism Management 13*, 267–74.

[48] **Kim**, H & Richardson, S. (2003) Motion Picture Impacts on Destination Images. *Annals of Tourism Research, 30*, 216–237.

[49] **Connell**, J. (2004) Toddlers, Tourism and Tobermory: Destination Marketing Issues and Television-Induced Tourism. *Tourism Management*, 26, 763–776.

[50] **Beeton**, S. (2005) *Film-Induced Tourism*. Channel View: Clevedon UK.

[51] **Interview with Forks Visitor Centre representatives**, Forks Washington, USA [16th of March 2011].

[52] **Cloudberry Communications** (2011) *Milleniumrapporten: Ekonomiska effekter av Stockholmregionen i de svenska Millenniumfilmerna.* Rapport på uppdrag av Filmregion Stockholm-Mälardalen, Regionförbundet Sörmland, Film i Sörmland och Stockholm Business Region Development.

[53] **Beeton**, S. (2010) The Advance of Film Tourism. *Tourism and Hospitality Planning & Development*, 7(1), 1–6.

[54] **Beeton**, S., (2006) Understanding Film-induced Tourism. *Tourism Analysis*, 11(3), 181–188.

Fans, fandoms and Twilight

"They are a very unique fanbase/…/it's a wonderful fanbase/…/The best way that I would explain the Twilight fanbase is that they are enthusiastic. Their enthusiasm is amazing and super infectious. It is very easy for mainstream culture to write off Star Trek fans, Star Wars fans, Harry Potter fans as "freaks"/…/But Twilight fans are a unique breed. There's no bitterness, there's no hatred, there's no jealousy amongst them. They are a very welcoming group. They love it when new Twilight fans come and join in. They are very patient with people who know nothing about Twilight. They are very eager to share their books, and 'this is why I love it so much'/…/The Twilight fanbase is still going to be very powerful in 40, 50, 60 years from now/…/I hope, sincerely, that 50, 60, 70 years from now the fanbase is still as pure, and sweet, and welcoming as it is now. That's my hope."

Larry Carrol, MTV News on Twilight fandom[1]

The majority of us have a fairly clear picture of what a fan is when we talk about them; typical associations are to a person with a deep involvement with, for example, a celebrity, film, television series or pop band, a person who possesses a great deal of information about his or her area of interest. However, within academia there is no generally accepted definition of fan or fandom, or of the neighbouring concept of fan cult, but all of these terms are usually linked to definitions that deal with enthusiasts to some form and degree, with different fan identities and experiences, who gather and are organised around a common interest.[2] Other definitions have focused on the emotional intensity, or affect, that characterises fans and fandom's relation to their area of interest.[3] In addition there is usually a regular and repeated consumption of this interest.

Twilight fans about to attend a Twilight promotion event in Stockholm, Sweden.

A popular image of fans in the media is a person who is obsessed with an interest or a celebrity; in the latter case the fan is often a person with mental health problems who stalks the celebrity. This image is a long way from the great majority of individuals who fall within the scope of the definitions presented by the concepts of fans and fandom, and who are commonly found in contemporary society:

> *"fandom seems to have become a common and ordinary aspect of everyday life in the industrialized world"*[4]

The central theme in the research around fans and fandoms is the power relationship or resistance between a group of fans and all the other non-fans. For example, this can be expressed by the fans' own interpretations that differ from the rest of the audience of a film, book or television series. It can also take the form of fans' consumption of their area of interest representing a contrast to their everyday lives:

> *"an activity and space far from the domestic pressures that otherwise structure the everyday life/…/a source of pleasure as well as emancipation and empowerment."*[5]

Other central themes in this area are community, identity and fandom as a social network and an extension of the self. The community between the fans and the comradeship in fandoms between people with the same interest have been covered in research literature. These social networks and the often very active participation by and between the members has been documented both on-line and in "real life".[6] This active participation in creation and co-creation is typical of the current postmodern era.[7] As regards research into fans' identities and fandoms as an extension of the self, they have been treated as an expression and release for the individual's pleasure and narcissism.[8] Additionally, the fans' travels to places have been discussed and similarities found with pilgrimages with religious undertones.[9]

The Twilight Saga as a pop culture phenomenon

One of the main explanations for Twilight's huge popularity with a large and international group of fans, mostly comprising women aged 8–80, is that this popularity lies in Twilight's opposing messages that include a traditionally conservative content mixed with modern values:

> *"a series that presents neither a subversive nor a conservative view of larger social contexts but is an ambiguous mixture of both/…/provides such narrative pleasure because it is able to offer different things to different readers. It is like a Vegas buffet – there is something for everyone"*[10]

Additional explanations have been presented, that deal with the story's ability to offer a secure refuge in the age that we are in, as well as keeping in tune with the fixation on the body that characterises this era:

> *"Edward is also a monster perfectly fitting for our post-9/11, anxiety-ridden age/…/promise that love can conquer all – even terrorist-like Volturi vampires/…/The vampires are 'the perfect being for our youth – and body obsessed era, signifying that we can indeed achieve corporeal perfection'"*[11]

Twilight fulfils the criteria that are normally given for a pop culture phenomenon. It is not just a book series that has sold more than 116 million copies[12] and generated more than USD 3.1 billion in cinema ticket and DVD sales[13]; a number of books/book series (e.g. *Night Huntress Series/World Series* (2008–), *Anna Strong Series* (2006–), *Vampire Academy Series* (2007–), films (e.g. *Daybreakers*, 2009; *Priest*, 2001; a new version of *Fright Night*, 2011) and television series (e.g. *Vampire*

Diaries (2009–), *True Blood* (2008–)[1])[14] have seen the light of day and achieved success as a consequence of Twilight's popularity. Vampires have become associated with automatic success and financial gain.

Our perceptions of vampires have changed, from blood thirsty, unpleasant and deathly *Nosferatu* to glittering, metrosexual, educated and beautiful beings.[15] Natalie Wilson describes the modern vampire in the following manner:

> *"usually a tortured outcast, a lonely immortal longing for love, family and approval/…/gorgeous creatures, their ice-cold ultra-white bodies not off-putting and corpselike but incarnations of the body beautiful; they are more Greek god than revivified corpse."*[16]

A number of bands and their songs have also been linked to Twilight, both via soundtracks to the films and as the playlists which the author Stephenie Meyer used when she wrote the books and which she has shared with her fans[17], and the fans' own playlists that they associate with Twilight and have shared with other fans.[18] A number of bands have reached new audiences thanks to the Twilight phenomenon, such as Stephenie Meyer's favourite group Muse, which she used for inspiration when writing.[19] Bands such as Paramore, Bon Iver, Florence + The Machine and Sweden's Lykke Li, among others, have also reached a new and larger market due to their contributions to the films' soundtracks.

Another example that illustrates Twilight as a pop culture phenomenon is its influence on fashion. Clothes such as tight t-shirts, hoodies and flannel shirts have rarely been as popular as after the film series' most popular actors started wearing them. Brands such as Penshoppe, Bench, BNY and Wrangler

---

[1] These, however, had been published as books before Twilight was published.

Jeans have even developed clothing lines influenced by the story's main characters.[20] Twilight's effect on fashion can also been seen on various blogs, where fans write about how they have changed their appearance due to their interest.[II]

> *"I've always loved to dress like Bella anyways- jeans, casual shirts, Converse are my favorite, and American Eagle was my favorite store. However when I turned 28 and my oldest started school, I started to dress "older". Button up shirts, dress shoes, and khakis. I secretly hated it, but didn't tell anyone. Now, I wear my Converse and am proud! I don't care anymore! It is my style – and I'm going back to it and loving it! It is going to shock the stuffy people I live around. Life is too short to live someone else's expectations!"*[21]

Another participant on the blog describes how she feels that others may react to her new way of dressing:

> *"I keep thinking that someone from "What Not To Wear" is going to jump out and tell me that these t-shirts are not appropriate attire for a 41 year old - but I don't care. I feel good when I wear them and I was not a t-shirt person before this."*[22]

Other fans talk about how they don't just choose a new clothes style for themselves, but also for those around them:

[II] The quotes come from the discussion forums on www.twilightmoms.com. To participate in these forums at least one of the following criteria must be fulfilled: 1) at least 18 years old, 2) be married or 3) have children. These forums have been used in order to demonstrate that it is not only youths that the Twilight phenomenon has affected in a range of ways.

"I found a dress that looks like the one Bella wore to prom I hope to purchase it soon. And I plan to buy a grey pea coat and blue button up shirt [like Edward wears] for my husband."[23]

Many people describe how they have changed their hairstyles or makeup, for example, inspired by various Twilight characters. A number of stories are presented here:

" I used to color my hair w/auburn coloring, now it's more milk chocolate like Bella's and I'm growing it long/.../I got my hair trimmed last week. It was short anyway. I find I am making it more messy looking to show off the razor cut layers in it. Alice and I have a similar hair style. That makes me smile/.../I've been thinking of wearing the fabric stretchy headbands *like the ones Jessica wears in the movie* My hair is darkish brown with blonde highlights seems fitting/.../Can't believe I am admitting to this! I LOVE being tan!!!! Like in a bad way. I do not over do it and look fakey orange ever, I am mainly tan in the summer. I have been doing my foundation light lately, rose lips. I love it. I am gonna do it until someone makes the comment that I look like a vampire/.../Apparently I'm not alone and vampire is in this year."[24]

The vast majority of stories about how Twilight has changed fans' appearances deal with how they have gained new energy and inspiration for training and weight loss:

" I think that my decision to get back in shape was TOTALLY Edward based....how completely mental is that!?!/.../I have lost about 13 lbs!!! My husband is thrilled...no word from Edward yet...../.../Last summer I lost 15 pounds! I did not care about anything but

reading, even when I was finished with all the books. I would go to the gym for an excuse to be able to read alone and not have the kids bother me. I could do an hour on the elliptical machine while reading and it would feel like 5 minutes! I also felt some sort of renewed spark of energy in my life/…/I also decided to go vegetarian, since.... well Edward is of course !/…/I like to call it my Twilight diet...and I am spreading the word to all my friends."[25]

As illustrated by the above quotes, Twilight fans spend a large amount of money on their interest, buying everything from posters, calendars, dolls, DVDs, soundtracks, iPods with Twilight games and applications to travel in the form of flights to and accommodation at Twilight destinations:

"I haven't got nearly as much as I'd like. My sweetie thinks I already have too much/…/So I am still on a quest to get more Twilight things for my display. There will never be an end. I have Books. Candy. Posters. Calendars. Dolls. Both DVD's... you know the usual stuff/…/ First let's start with my i-Phone, I have all 4 books downloaded from Iceburg Reader, all 4 also on audio, both soundtracks, both movies, the Twilight Tracker app, Twilight & New Moon trivia games. At home I have 2 sets of books, one paperback and one hardcover set, trading cards, both DVD's and both Blue Ray copies of the movies/…/Plus, I went to Forks and Portland last year which was awesome/…/I spent basically $1 000 on a flight to Seattle (from the UK) for my upcoming Forks trip, and that's before I even get there, pay accommodation etc... I don't even want to start adding on to that for how much I've spent going to conventions, buying merch..."[26]

Many of them admit that they have spent large amounts of money on their interest:

> " I think the amounts would scare me. I buy something Twilight every weekend almost so the money amount must be over six or seven hundred at least. I'm afraid it might be much more/…/ I would hate to know how much I have spent/…/ I'm too scared to add up what I have spent on My twilight obsession…its, ah, pretty bad."[27]

Some fans talk about the outside world's view of their Twilight-related consumption. Some meet resistance, while others have the support of those around them:

> "My hubby was suprized by the amount of $ for that 3D poster, but oh well. He has his playstation 3 and each new game costs from between $40–$60 each…so he can suck it up/…/my wonderful hubby puts it, it's better I put that money on Twilight than on bars, drugs or worse. At least I only spend my spare money and I get all the necessities before I splurge on my obsession/…/ My Twi friends are the same…I call ourselves 'teenagers with credit cards'. You know, I haven't had buyer's remorse at all… not for one single product I bought. I love all of them."[28]

We conducted a survey of Twilight fans in which they had to evaluate their interest and commitment to Twilight on a seven-point scale, and they assessed this as very high ($\bar{x}$ = 6.41). However, when they were asked whether Twilight was vital to them and thus how difficult it was to choose between Twilight and other hobbies, this was assessed as being much lower ($\bar{x}$ = 3.90). Similarly, few of the fans felt that the Twilight products they bought were either a reward ($\bar{x}$ = 3.65) or symbolised their personality and character ($\bar{x}$ = 3.59) (see below).[29]

Twilight fans' involvement with Twilight.
Scale: 1 = strongly disagree, 7 = strongly agree)

	Mean	n
I'm interested in Twilight	6.41	888
Twilight is essential to me, thus it is difficult to choose be tween Twilight and my other hobbies	3.90	899
Purchasing Twilight products is a way of rewarding myself	3.65	890
The Twilight products I purchase symbolize my personality and character	3.59	887

Twihards, Twifans, Twitans, Twilighters, Twiholics – a much loved child has many names!

Twilight has changed many people's lives in many ways. It was not only the author, Stephenie Meyers' life that changed practically overnight – from American housewife to bestselling multimillionaire and one of *Forbes'* "*10 Most Powerful Women Authors*" of 2011.[30] Summit Entertainment, which produced all the Twilight films, has also become a highly successful film production company as a result of its work with Twilight. Added to these are the actors who were relatively unknown before Twilight: Robert Pattinson, Kristin Stewart (both listed by *Forbes* in 2011 in the category of "*Best Paid Celebrities Under 30*"[31]), Taylor Lautner and others, who are now ranked among the 'hottest' Hollywood celebrities. Fans also testify to how Twilight has changed their lives, with some talking about a newly awakened interest in literature:

"It pretty much changed OUR LIVES, in the sense that we developed our fervor for reading. Started from reading this whole SAGA, and now you're finishing up a whole lot of other books. That's so COOL."[32]

As previously mentioned, volumes of fiction about vampires have been produced and consumed by Twilight fans and others. Book series in other genres such as *The Hunger Games*[33] and *The Mortal Instruments*[34] have also been read, embraced and spread by Twilight fans, among others, and this has been central to the success of these book series. Both *The Hunger Games*[III] and *The Mortal Instruments* have been so successful that films are currently in production.[35]

A great deal of fan fiction has also been written on the theme of Twilight. Fan fiction[IV] comprises stories that are written by fans about the characters in books, television series, films and comics. Often these are not approved by the copyright holder and are rarely published in traditional forms, but are instead distributed on internet forums, such as www.fanfiction.net, or in fanzines[V]. These stories may either follow the canonised fictional universe created by the copyright holder, or the characters are placed in an alternative universe. In the case of Twilight, this may mean that all the characters are human instead of vampires and werewolves, and are located in Britain in the Middle Ages, for example. The majority of fan fiction writers assume that the readers of their texts are primarily other fans who are therefore familiar with the canonical universe of the original. Popular stories about which a lot of fan fiction has been presented over the years are *Star Trek, Star Wars, Harry*

[III] The first movie in the series has been released.

[IV] Also called fanfiction, fanfic, FF and fic.

[V] Unofficial publications that are produced by fans about a specific cultural phenomenon.

Potter and now Twilight. In recent years, some authors, such as J.K. Rowling (author of the Harry Potter books), have said that they are flattered that fans want to create their own stories based on their characters. Another example is that of Stephenie Meyer, who says that she reads Twilight fan fiction and has put links on her website to other websites on which fan fiction is published.[36]

A number of the fan fiction stories that are based on Twilight and which have reached large audiences on various fan fiction forums have then been published as books by traditional publishers (e.g. Omnific, The Writer's Coffee Shop Publishing House, The Wild Rose Press). In these cases, the characters' names and, in some cases, histories have been changed to avoid copyright disputes. As many as 52 former Twilight fan fiction stories have been published in traditional book form, according to an established organisation in Twilight fandom.[37] This form of publication is notable, as in many cases the stories have had a readership during the time they were being created and published on the internet (WIP = Work in Progress). As a result of this, the author has received feedback from his or her readership during the story's production, which can be described as a postmodern co-creation of a product. A controversial example of this is a former Twilight fanfiction story published as the trilogy *50 Shades of Grey*. It has not only become a bestselling book series worldwide but the author herself is included in Time's list of "The 100 Most Influential People in the World".[38] In addition to this, Universal Pictures and Focus Features have acquired screen rights to the series.[39]

As previously mentioned, the recreation of meaning in pop culture can be expressed as *fan productivity*, as the above example of fan fiction demonstrates. However, this form of productivity is also exemplified by the writing of new music or the formation of new bands inspired by Twilight.[40] Another example is that of technophobes who learn how to use new software to create pictures and videos based on the phenomenon.

A number of these productive fans become famous personalities within the fan culture, known as Super Fandom People (SFP), as both they and their works are voted for via annual competitions.[41] Another example of productivity in Twilight fan culture, and an indication of how organised this fandom is, is the number of charity projects that are linked to it. The charity work that is conducted is primarily focused on a range of illnesses and related research (e.g. Fandom for the Leukemia & Lymphoma Society, Fandom Fights Mental Illness), as well as contemporary disasters (e.g. Fandom Fights the Tsunamis, Fandoms Fight The Floods). Perhaps the best known of these is *Alex's Lemonade Stand: Foundation for Childhood Cancer* which one of the lead actors in the Twilight films also supports. One of these charity organisations, *Fandom Gives Back,* has raised around USD 240,000 since it started.[42] Another indication of the level of organisation in fan culture is the planning of various types of Twilight-related events, which can be found on numerous websites and blogs, as well as the competitions that are organised by the fans themselves, in different genres of fan fiction.[43]

The sense of community among the Twilight fans is something that characterises their fandom and which is described as something highly significant and that changes their lives. One important prerequisite of this sense of community is the interaction between the fans on the internet:

> *"I'm really thankful about this. THE TWILIGHT SAGA HELPED ME GAIN, MEET AND KNOW LOTS OF PEOPLE. I've meet and known a lot of PE-OPLE, not just LOCALLY but INTERNATIONAL-LY. With that I am so thankful and happy. Now, I get to have friends that I can talk to about anything in particular. It's like THE TWILIGHT SAGA, became a bridge for knowing lots of people. And I really treasure this people that I've met because of TWILIGHT. I really will."*[44]

Many people say that the communal feeling among a group of like-minded fans on the internet has given them an understanding of their own reactions and feelings after reading the books or seeing the films:

> *"When I first started the books I thought there was something mentally wrong with me. Seriously! Then I found Twilight Moms (thank you!) and am happy to read that others are trying to make sense of this fascination for Stephenie Meyer's world./…/ It's nice to know there is an explanation to all this! Instead of just labeling us CRAZY!"*[45]

For many of the fans who share their experiences on forums and blogs, Twilight has had a marked influence on their lives. Some talk about how they have found the strength to change their lives in areas where they were previously dissatisfied:

> *"I feel like I'm my 'old self'" again. I not only revamp*[VI] *the books all the time, I am now obsessed with this site, too/…/I was in a really bad marriage. I knew it was over and that it was time to divorce. But I was scared to move forward and feeling pretty hopeless. I really feel that Twilight somehow gave me back some hope for a future. I think it's important though to realize that no human man can really be Edward - or even Jacob. I worried for a while that I was ruined - and could only be happy with a non-existent vampire... but I'm beyond all of that now and actually happily dating a very human man/…/ I was in an iffy relationship when I read Twilight, and I am SO glad I read it!! It helped me to see the truth about my ex - that he was very very selfish*

[VI] Revamp = rereading the Twilight books.

and treated me badly. Now I've found someone, and while it is still new, I feel just like Bella did when she and Edward started seeing each other."[46]

Other fans talk about how Twilight has made them start to appreciate the lives they live, to live in the present moment and to regain the passion in their lives:

"I appreciate these books so much because they really brought back the love and passion in my relationship (married 16 years)/…/The Twilight Series came on my radar at definitely the right time when I needed some escapism and fun fantasy. I've read and re-read them more times than I'd ever admit to. The series made me realize just how much I was neglecting 'me' in my life.... So I redirected my life and best of all I like me a whole lot better/…/Twilight came into my life when I was just going through the daily motions and routines. It brought passion back into my life. I have found that I love to read and it is just for me. My marriage is just there. No emotion attached after 29 years. It is sad to say he just doesn't seem care. But I have come to terms with it and I am rediscovering thing that make me happy. Twilight opened this door for me and now I do not hesitate to try new things and meet new people. Twilight may be fiction, but it woke up excitement back into my life. And life is too short not to make the most of it."[47]

Some fans describe their interest in Twilight as practically being a form of obsession:

"Like you all, I was obsessed with this series. LOVED them beyond belief. Felt Bella's feelings and lived it all right there with her. Felt her joy at the end of BD when

she was able to share her mind with Edward. It was a
beautiful, magical, amazingly written series."[48]

Many of them liken their relationship with the phenomenon to that of being at the falling in love stage of a relationship. One fan puts this to her peers on a Twilight blog, in an attempt to understand their shared emotions:

"Have you experienced a dramatic shift in consciousness in that this "obsession" has taken on a special meaning and become all-important? Have you focused all of your attention on Twilight, often to the detriment of everything and everyone around you, including work, family and friends? Have you concentrated on all of the events, songs, and other little things that you associate with Twilight? Do you replay these things in your mind's eye as you muse about Twilight? Have you experienced obsessive meditation about Twilight; something called "intrusive thinking". You can't get Twilight out of your mind? Have you experienced a loss of appetite and/or sleeplessness?/…/So in answer to some of the questions I asked myself when I first read these books; I have literally fallen in love with Twilight. I am truly experiencing the same reactions to this book as one has when falling in love with another person."[49]

Some of them find the explanation for their feelings about the Twilight phenomenon in the chemical reactions in the body when a person falls in love, as do these two fans of the series - a psychologist and a molecular biologist:

"Now I understand part of why I have had all of these strange responses to reading a book. But my next question is 'why?' Why am I acting as though I were an 18 year old falling in love? What is causing these reactions?

43

My theory has been that it is chemically related. Well, it seems to follow that the same chemical reactions that cause these behaviors when we are falling in love are probably those that are causing these responses to Twilight. Some of the main chemicals that have been studied in the roles they play in romantic love are dopamine, norepinephrine, and serotonin/…/I am a molecular biologist and it is /[nice to]…/hear the biology explained from a psychologist's point of view. I wonder what genes are involved (just those responsible for hormone production and signaling?). If a guy gave these books a chance, would he also 'fall in love' with Twilight or is his biochemistry all wrong?"[50]

Many fans use quotes from the books and films, with an ironic edge, to draw likenesses between their obsession with the phenomenon:

"Stephenie Meyer's Twilight Saga.... It's like A drug to me.. it's my own personal brand of heroine[VII]*."*[51]

Some fans say that when they have finished reading the books, they experience a type of depression similar to that experienced when a relationship ends:

"I was a wreck after I finished the Saga. I wasn't myself for a couple days and my family definitely knew something was wrong w/me. They never knew the extent of my emotional state. I was lucky enough to have the days to myself and cope with all the real feelings I was experiencing. I realized that I had to remember my life

[VII] In the Twilight film, the original is: *"It's like a drug to me. It's like you're my own personal brand of heroin."*

pre-Twilight and just hold on to those feelings/…/All I can liken it to is a mini-depression or a real & serious mid-life crisis."[52]

Psychologist Louise Deacon writes about the 'risks' of exposure to Twilight's powerfully romantic message in her book *Twilight, True Love and You: Seven Secret Steps to Finding Your Edward or Jacob*. The book relates the main character Bella's experiences of falling in love, and love itself, to the reader's actual relationships.[53]

Twi-talk – a shared language

A common phenomenon among different fan cultures is the development of a shared language, or words that are used as codes for central concepts within the shared area of interest. This is an expression of the sense of belonging and community that a fan culture can represent.[54] Many of the expressions that are found within the Twilight fan culture are related to a feeling or behaviour that is associated with the phenomenon:

"**Twitten**: *Reading the first book and getting bitten by the Twilight bug. The inexplicable force that drove us to read all the books in (practically) one sitting/…/* **Twitchcraft**: *Type of magic spell put on the Twilight Saga, once someone opens the book they are completely in love and obsessed with all things related to it/…/* **Twiloholic** - *A name for your addiction to everything Twilight/…/* **OCD** – *Obsessive Cullen Disorder/…/* **Twimmersing/Tweference**: *Tying everything to Twilight by any means necessary/…/* **Twilingial** – *incorporating 'Twilight' language into your everyday speech.* **Revamp**: *Reading the books again. And again. And again!/…/* **Twilaphobia** *the fear of not having the Twilight books with you at all times so they can be read or referenced at a moment's notice/…/* **Twanxious** – *the feeling you*

45

get while waiting for the next instalment of Twilight... book release dates, movie release dates, etc./... ***Post-Saga Depression (PSD)****: The blue feeling after finishing the books and realizing there is no actual Edward.*"[55]

Others are clearly associated with the fictional characters' traits or behaviours:

> "***Bella moment*** *last weekend while walking to my car. I had my hands full, stepped in a pothole, and totally fell on my knees. I ripped my jeans in the process! Grrr!* ***Total Bella Moment!****/.../****Edwardian****: A term used when a husband does not behave or respond appropriately. For example, 'that wasn't very Edwardian of you.'*"[56]

Some expressions are used to mark important dates in the fan culture, such as:

> "***BfTW*** *(Before Twilight) and* ***TWE*** *(Twilight Era)/.../* ***Twi-versary****... the anniversary of the day you started reading Twilight for the first time.*"[57]

Words for physical expressions of the consumption of this pop culture phenomenon are also common:

> "***Twibrary*** *- Your collection of all things related to Twilight, including books, movies, etc./...I bought an ipod touch solely for Twilight related stuff, I call mine my* ***Twi-touch****/...*/***TwiCrack****: Twilight-related news, information and memorabilia that fuels burning Twilight addictions for those who are* ***High on Twi*** *(-light, that is)/...*/***Twi-llowance****: the portion of my monthly budget dedicated toward Twilight-related purchases*"[58]

References

[1] **Destination Forks**: The Real World of Twilight (2010) DVD, Summit Entertainment.

[2] **Hills**, M. (2002). *Fan Cultures,* Routledge, UK.

[3] **Grossberg**, L. (1992) "Is There a Fan in the House?: The Affective Sensibility of Fandom", in L.A. Lewis (Ed) *The Adoring Audience,* Routledge: London.
Sandvoss, C. (2005) *Fans*, Polity Press, UK.

[4] **Sandvoss**, C. (2005) *Fans*, Polity Press, UK, p. 3.

[5] **Sandvoss**, C. (2005) *Fans*, Polity Press, UK, p. 19.

[6] **Hills**, M. (2002) *Fan Cultures,* Routledge, UK.
Jenkins, H. (2006) *Fans, Bloggers and Gamers: Exploring Participatory Culture*. New York University Press: USA.

[7] **Lusch**, R. F., & Vargo, S. L. (2006) Service-Dominant Logic as a Foundation for Building a General Theory. In R. F. Lusch, & S. L. Vargo (Eds.), *The Service-Dominant Logic of Marketing: Dialog, Debate and Directions*. Armonk: New York, p. 406–420.
Vargo, S. L., & Lusch, R. F. (2004) Evolving to a New Dominant Logic for Marketing. *Journal of Marketing, 68*(1), 1–17.
Etgar, M. (2008) A Descriptive Model of the Consumer Co-Production Process. *Journal of the Academy of Marketing Science, 36,* 97–108.

[8] **Sandvoss**, C. (2005) *Fans*, Polity Press, UK.

[9] **Aden**, R.C. (1999) *Popular Stories and Promised Lands: Fan Culture and Symbolic Pilgrimages.* University of Alabama Press: Tuscaloosa and London.
Sandvoss, C. (2005) *Fans*, Polity Press, UK.
Hills, M. (2002) *Fan Cultures,* Routledge, UK.

[10] **Wilson**, N. (2011) *Seduced by Twilight: The Allure and Contradictory Messages of the Popular Saga,* McFarland & Company Inc, Jefferson, US, p. 8.

[11] **Wilson**, N. (2011). *Seduced by Twilight: The Allure and Contradictory Messages of the Popular Saga,* McFarland & Company Inc, Jefferson, USA, p. 34–35.

[12] **http://www.publishersweekly.com/pw/by-topic/childrens/childrens-book-news/article/44733-little-brown-to-publish-official-twilight-guide.html** [Retrieved: 17th of September 2012]

[13] **www.the-numbers.com**

[14] **www.IMBd.com**

[15] **Banzuela**, A. www.robstenphilippines.blogspot.com/ [Retrieved: 26th of February 2011].

[16] **Wilson**, N. (2011) *Seduced by Twilight: The Allure and Contradictory Messages of the Popular Saga,* McFarland & Company Inc, Jefferson, USA, p. 16.

[17] **http://www.stepheniemeyer.com/** [Retrieved: 26th of February 2011]

[18] **Banzuela**, A. www.robstenphilippines.blogspot.com/ [Retrieved: 26th of February 2011]

[19] **http://www.stepheniemeyer.com**/twilightseries.html [Retrieved: 26th of February 2011]

[20] **Banzuela**, A. www.robstenphilippines.blogspot.com/ [Retrieved: 26th of February 2011]

[21] **www.twilightmoms.com** Forum: "Have you changed the way you look or dress?" Years: 2008–2011

[22] **www.twilightmoms.com** Forum: "Have you changed the way you look or dress?" Years: 2008–2011

[23] **www.twilightmoms.com** Forum: "Have you changed the way you look or dress?" Years: 2008–2011

[24] **www.twilightmoms.com** Forum: "Have you changed the way you look or dress?" Years: 2008–2011

[25] **www.twilightmoms.com** Forum: "Have you changed the way you look or dress?" Years: 2008–2011

[26] **www.twilightmoms.com** Forum: "How much have you spent?" Years: 2010–2011

[27] **www.twilightmoms.com** Forum: "How much have you spent?" Years: 2010–2011

[28] **www.twilightmoms.com** Forum: "How much have you spent?" Years: 2010–2011

[29] **International web survey** on "Twilight, tourism and social media" ETOUR Mid Sweden University. Contact: Christine Lundberg (Christine.Lundberg@miun.se)

[30] **Twilight Examiner**: http://www.examiner.com/twilight-in-national/stephenie-meyer-makes-forbes-10-most-powerful-women-authors-list [Retrieved: 9th of June 2011]

[31] **http://www.forbes.com**/2011/06/09/top-earning-celebrities-under-30_slide_18.html

[32] **Banzuela**, A. www.robstenphilippines.blogspot.com/ [Retrieved: 26th of February 2011]

[33] **http://www.suzannecollinsbooks.com/** [Retrieved: 9th of June 2011]

[34] **http://www.mortalinstruments.com/** [Retrieved: 9th of June 2011]

[35] **Hunger Games**: http://www.imdb.com/title/tt1392170/ [Retrieved: 9th of June 2011]

Mortal Instruments: http://www.imdb.com/title/tt1538403/ [Retrieved: 9th of June 2011]

[36] **http://en.wikipedia.org**/wiki/Fan_fiction [Retrieved: 10th of June 2011]

[37] **http://published.thetwilightawards.com/** [Retrieved: 10th of June 2011]

[38] **http://www.time.com/**time/specials/packages/completelist/0,29569,2111975,00.html [Retrieved: 1st of June 2012]

[39] **http://www.deadline.com**/2012/03/universal-pictures-and-focus-features-win-50-shades-of-grey/ [Retrieved: 1st of June 2012]

[40] **Destination Forks**: The Real World of Twilight (2010) DVD, Summit Entertainment.

[41] **http://www.thetwilightawards.com/** [Retrieved: 10th of June 2011]

[42] **www.twitter.com** Tweet from @fandomgivesback [Retrieved: 7th of June 2011]

[43] **http://www.thetwilightawards.com/** [Retrieved: 10th of June 2011]

[44] **Banzuela**, A. www.robstenphilippines.blogspot.com/ [Retrieved: 26th of February 2011]

[45] **www.twilightmoms.com** Forum: "What has happened to us?! Some logical explanations" Years: 2009–2011

[46] **www.twilightmoms.com** Forum: "What has happened to us?! Some logical explanations" Years: 2009–2011

[47] **www.twilightmoms.com** Forum: "What has happened to us?! Some logical explanations" Years: 2009–2011

[48] **www.twilightmoms.com** Forum: "What has happened to us?! Some logical explanations" Years: 2009–2011

[49] **www.twilightmoms.com** Forum: "What has happened to us?! Some logical explanations" Years: 2009–2011

[50] **www.twilightmoms.com** Forum: "What has happened to us?! Some logical explanations" Years: 2009–2011

[51] **www.twilightmoms.com** Forum: "What has happened to us?! Some logical explanations" Years: 2009–2011

[52] **www.twilightmoms.com** Forum: "What has happened to us?! Some logical explanations" Years: 2009–2011

[53] **http://www.summersdale.com**/book/2/478/twilight-true-love-and-you/

[54] **Sandvoss**, C. (2005) *Fans*, Polity Press, UK.
Hills, M. (2002) *Fan Cultures,* Routledge, UK.

[55] **www.twilightmoms.com** Forum: "Twilight terms for our Twilight Dictionary" Years: 2008–2011

[56] **www.twilightmoms.com** Forum: "Twilight terms for our Twilight Dictionary" Years: 2008–2011

[57] **www.twilightmoms.com** Forum: "Twilight terms for our Twilight Dictionary" Years: 2008–2011

[58] **www.twilightmoms.com** Forum: "Twilight terms for our Twilight Dictionary" Years: 2008–2011

Twicationers™ – Twilight fans as tourists

"We are on a pilgrimage; we are on a pilgrimage to Forks/…/It's crazy to be here…like a place where Jesus walked on water"

Twilight fans on their visit to Forks, Washington,
USA and British Columbia, Canada.

Who are the fans who travel to destinations to experience the phenomenon that interests them? According to our international web survey, the majority are women.[1] Unlike the stereotypical media image of Twilight fans as teenage girls, many of the fans who travel are more mature women. Teenagers do comprise the single largest group (38 per cent), but the remaining 62 per cent are 20 years old or above, with the oldest documented Twilight tourist aged 68.[1] These Twilight fans, who travel as part of their fan experience, are a reflection of the Twilight fandom as a whole that has participated in the study, where the fans' age distribution is similar (19 and younger: 38%; 20–29: 30%; 30–39: 16%; 40–49: 10% and 50 or above: 6%)[II].

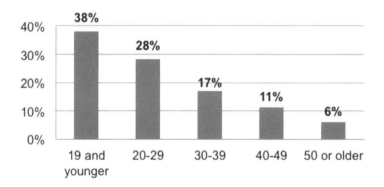

---

[1] *n=491*

[II] *n=854*

Tourist operators at the Twilight destinations also confirm that both men and women, but primarily women who are older than the stereotype, visit the destinations. The visitor center in Forks, Washington, describes the visitor groups:

> "NOT teenage girls/.../our fans is [sic] getting older and older! And it is not only women anymore, we have men fans too. I think that is wonderful, I do not know what it is about the books, I do not know if it is the best written book in the world or if she is the finest author. But she certainly tells a story that people want to know about."

Despite the majority of fans being women, there are a number of men who visit both the film sites and the places described in the book. One tour operator in Vancouver, Canada, describes the visitors in the following manner:

> "They are mostly girls but I do get a lot of guys/.../ I do have husbands, boyfriends, dads, grandpas, uncles, I had uncles taking their nieces on trips, I have dads coming with daughters, had grandfathers coming."

Some of the men who visit the Twilight destinations don't want to admit that they are Twilight fans. An owner of accommodation in Forks, Washington, describes this:

> "So there aren't as many men that we see that come and admit to being fans – I am doing this for my wife, I am doing this for my daughter."

Representatives from the Twilight destinations believe that one explanation for the more mature visitor group is that this is the age group that can afford the trips, which are sometimes expensive. One tour operator describes this in the following way:

Welcome sign at the border between Forks and La Push, WA, USA, Also known among Twilight fans as the Treaty-Line between vampires and werewolves.

"I had a surgeon come from Florida, very wealthy, she was surgeon and she brought her mom and dad up to Vancouver and the majority are women over 35 that have children and work. Because they need money to come here and they love Twilight and they love the [Twilight] Saga and they get some friends together and they come/…/The price of the tour is not cheap. But also to come to Vancouver and to stay in a hotel and travel here…you have to have some money to do that because Vancouver is very expensive."

At the tourist office in Volterra, Italy, they have had the same experience of older visitor groups:

"When we started to work on that [Twilight tourism] two years ago, we were like, sure it's going to be teenagers between 13 and 17/…/So we were actually really wrong about that/…/So they're actually much older."

Mother and daughter visit the film location for Twilight: Breaking Dawn Part 1 and 2, in Squamish, British Columbia, Canada.

In the neighbouring town of Montepulciano, which is one of the locations for film number 2 in the series, New Moon, the town's media and tourism development manager says that many teenagers and their mothers visit to experience Twilight, particularly during filming:

> *"most of the people/.../were teenagers, but not only, there are also their mums, that come not just for their sons and daughters, but just for themselves."*

They are also a well-educated group of tourists, of which 59 per cent[III] have completed some form of higher education.[2] This distribution is representative of all Twilight fans (those who travel because of Twilight and those who don't) who participated in the survey.[IV] The staff at the tourist office in Volterra also

---

[III] $n=485$
[IV] $n=838$

find them to be well-educated, as they make a connection between their ages and the products they are interested in buying on their visit to the destination:

> "they are very…very educated/…/there is no fan shop, for example, there is no shop just selling merchandising… industrial merchandising/…/[they sell] things for New Moon on alabaster, for example, there are those alabaster bowls for example."

These older, more educated tourists are also described as more interested in the actual process of filming than in seeing the actors when they visit the locations, according to a tour operator in Vancouver:

> "I think older people are more interested in the behind the scenes and the process/…/a lot of people are interested about how do they [production company] find the spots, that is always the big question, how did they find Jacob's house and how did they find the woods/…/I don't think/[younger fans]/care that much, I think they more care about what Edward looked like when I saw him."

The tourist industry believes that, in addition to seeing the actors in the films and gaining insight into the filming processes, visiting the Twilight locations offers readers/viewers a "happy place" in troubled times, a kind of refuge from grim reality, that they want to experience when they visit the destinations. The staff at the visitor center in Forks summarise this in the following manner:

> "we live in a troubled world, there is a lot of scary stuff out there. It is nice to have something that romantic and wonderful and it is imagination and we know

that it is not real but it gives people something to think about. Escaping the reality. They are making an adventure when they come here and they come back, they do."

The Twilight Saga as a reason to travel

From a destination perspective, it is particularly interesting to know whether an attraction is a primary or secondary reason to travel for visiting tourists. A large number, 67 per cent, of Twilight fans say that they have travelled 1 to 4 times with Twilight as their primary reason for travel. Seven per cent say that they have travelled 10 times or more with Twilight as their primary reason to travel.[v] Of these trips, 66 per cent were 1 to 4 domestic trips[vi], while 29 per cent comprised 1 to 4 international trips.[vii] The staff members at the tourist office in Volterra testify to the international side of Twilight tourism, as their destination received visitors from all around the world due to Twilight:

> *"Concerning countries, it's a mixture of everywhere, so they come from all over the world from Singapore, Japan, Russia, America of course, Australia, and then all Europe, also now from Czech Republic..."*

25 per cent of Twilight fans have travelled with Twilight as a secondary reason to travel 1 to 4 times.[viii] Of these trips, 45 per cent, they made 1 to 4 as domestic trips[ix], while only 18 per cent comprised 1 to 4 international trips.[x] It is notable, and of central importance for destination development, that 65 per cent of the Twilight tourists would not have visited the destination they did if it wasn't for Twilight.[xi] We have chosen to call

---

[v] $n=945$
[vi] $n=912$
[vii] $n=916$
[viii] $n=693$
[ix] $n=725$
[x] $n=727$
[xi] $n=694$

this *Twilight Attractiveness* and, in practice, it means that tourists have chosen to visit entirely new destinations, which they would not otherwise have visited, if it wasn't for their interest in the pop culture phenomenon of Twilight.

The trip's construction – on organisation, journey length, companions and mode of transport

The result that shows that only 42 per cent state that they have used an organised form of travel, such as a travel agency or operator during their most recent Twilight trip, is of great relevance to the tourist industry. 56 per cent have organised their trip themselves, with family or close friends, and 26 per cent state that an online fan community has organised the trip.[XII] One example of online organised travel is Twitarded's annual trip to Forks (see photo below).

Fan organised travel on www.twitarded.blogspot.com ahead of the 2011 Stephenie Meyer Day in Forks, WA, US.[3]

[XII] $n=866$; the respondents could choose several alternatives.

Once at the destination, 84 per cent say that they do not choose to pay to participate in an organised package trip.[13] 11

All of these results indicate strongly fan-driven travel with little involvement from commercial players in the planning and organisation process. In our international internet survey, 11 per cent of the tourists could be categorised as destination tourists, i.e. tourists who travel to destinations clearly associated with Twilight, such as Forks in Washington, USA, British Columbia in Canada or Volterra and Montepulciano in Italy. The biggest category of Twilight travellers in the web survey is the event tourists (89 per cent), who visit different types of Twilight events around the world at destinations that are not specifically associated with Twilight. Examples of these include Comic Con in San Diego, Twilight marketing events, Twi-Cons (Twilight conventions), film premieres, talk shows and fan-organised events.[XIV]

55 per cent of travellers stated that their most recent Twilight trip lasted one day, while 28 per cent of the tourists' trips lasted 2 to 4 days.[XV] They primarily travel with real life (RL) friends, followed by family and a combination of family and friends.[XVI]

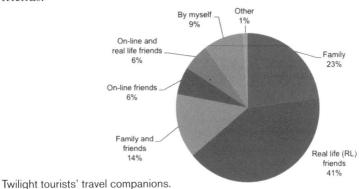

Twilight tourists' travel companions.

[XIII] $n=581$
[XIV] $n=592$
[XV] $n=668$
[XVI] $n=665$

Tourists dress as the Twilight characters Rosalie, Alice and Bella on their visit to Forks, WA, USA.

As regards the mode of travel, these tourists primarily chose to drive on their most recent Twilight trip. Air and rail were also popular. The choice of transport also indicates how far one travels and how accessible the destinations are to travellers, as regards varying modes of transport.[XVII]

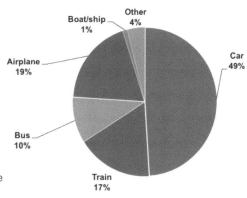

Twilight tourists' choice of transport.

Other 4%
Boat/ship 1%
Car 49%
Airplane 19%
Bus 10%
Train 17%

[XVII] $n=659$

Searching for and finding tourist information

There are many ways and places that can be used for searching for and finding tourist information when planning a trip. Traditional channels have been travel agents/operators, the destinations' own marketing material and recommendations from friends and relatives.[4] In recent years, the first two sources in particular have faced competition from the information that is shared and disseminated via the Internet, using more or less controlled forms and sources.[5] In film tourism, Frost[6] believes that fan tourists search for and find information about film tourism destinations by:

- Word of mouth
- Guidebooks about destinations
- Books about film
- Film maps/trails
- Traditional marketing material
- Attractions, tours
- Blogs
- Internet site: IMDB (Internet Movie Database)
- Special material on film DVDs

To a certain extent, these sources correspond to the Twilight tourists' choice of information sources. However, it is notable that 56 per cent have Twilight-related websites as the primary source of information when planning their trips. Other popular sources of information are other Internet sites (i.e. not Twilight-related) and social media (blogs and communities).

It is also startling that only 3 per cent use traditional travels agencies and operators as their primary source of information when they are looking for information about their trip.[XVIII] Overall, one can say that Twilight tourists primarily search for and value information from like-minded people on the Internet, i.e. other Twilight fans, when they are planning their trips.[7]

[XVIII] $n=643$

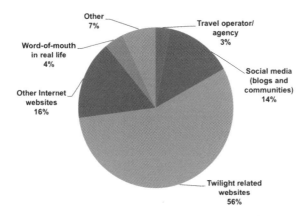

Twilight tourists' choice of information sources when planning trips.

Travel expenses

There are two extremes among Twilight tourists as regards the amount of money they spent during their most recent Twilight-related trip. 52 per cent state that they have spent up to USD 99 while 15 per cent have spent USD 1000 or more.[xix]

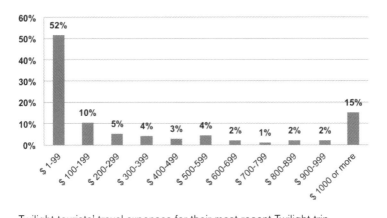

Twilight tourists' travel expenses for their most recent Twilight trip.

[xix] $n=505$

Why do Twilight tourists travel and what value do they experience?

Tourists' reasons to travel are traditionally divided into the categories "searching – escapism", "pull – push" and "personal rewards – interpersonal rewards". The first of these categories, "searching – escapism", deals with the tourist's desire to satisfy an internal need to either search for new experiences or to "flee" ordinary life by taking part in tourism activities. The second category, "push – pull", deals with the psychological and social processes within the tourist that lead him or her to travel: on the one hand, and on the other hand it deals with the receiving destination's attraction power that "pulls" the tourist to it.[8] Of the "personal – interpersonal rewards", the personal ones are relaxation, rest and self-fulfillment, while the interpersonal rewards primarily deal with social interactions with family, friends and other people.[9]

However, when describing Twilight tourists' reasons to travel, there is a need for more complex concepts that can explain the more complicated needs that underlie fan tourism, including a passionate interest in a specific phenomenon in which the person invests a great deal of time, money and energy: "*it cannot be reduced to a few basic drives and needs*".[10]

A great deal of the research into fan tourism has focused on sports fans and how they travel. These studies have shown that fans that identify strongly with an interest are more likely to participate in tourism activities, travel longer distances and spend more money on products:

> "*Fans with stronger identification have sport more deeply embedded in their self-concept, and are more likely to attend games and travel greater distances to do so, purchase merchandise, spend more on tickets and products, and remain loyal.*"[11]

Research in fan tourists' reasons for travel has divided these motivations into three different spheres: psychological, socio-cultural and social connections. Examples of psychological motivations are positive stress/excitement, escapism, aesthetic pleasure and drama and entertainment.[12] Sociocultural motivation includes time with family, friends and like-minded people (social interaction) and a cultural connection to what are often called mythical images, icons and symbols.[13]

Motivation in the sphere of social connections consists of tribal connections and vicarious achievement. The former deals with the experience of belonging to a clear group, a tribe, with shared norms, routines, symbols, rituals and language. The latter deals with the experience of sharing success and thus satisfaction through the link to a successful person or team.[14] In addition, there are a number of influencing factors that either reinforce or dampen these motivations; these are primarily demographic factors such as age, education, income, gender and ethnicity.[15]

When Twilight tourists were able to grade which reasons to travel were most important to them, they ranked the following highest:[16] *"to experience a Twilight atmosphere"* ($\bar{x}$ = 5.80), *"to participate in activities that are fun"* ($\bar{x}$ =5.76), *"to have fun with my friends and/or family"* ($\bar{x}$ = 5.70), *"to experience excitement"* ($\bar{x}$ =5.70) and *"to experience a sense of belongingness to Twilight and/or the Twilight community"* ($\bar{x}$ = 5.34).

The lowest ranked reasons to travel were: *"to party and drink"* ($\bar{x}$ = 2.13), *"to participate in other activities that are not Twilight related"* ($\bar{x}$ =2.88), *"to meet old friends"* ($\bar{x}$ =3.28), *"to visit an attractive destination"* ($\bar{x}$ = 3.66) and *"to have an opportunity to visit this particular destination"* ($\bar{x}$ =3.72).[xx]

These results paint a picture of Twilight tourists as being strongly motivated by the actual Twilight experience, such as atmosphere and belonging to the Twilight community, as well

---

[xx] Scale 1–7 used, n=546–578

September 28 - October 1, 2009

My mom and I came here to see Forks purely for the "Twilight" sights, but we enjoyed the area even without the "Twilight" influence. We saw the Hoh Rain Forest and Ruby Beach — both very beautiful. And of course we hit all the Twilight sights — The Swan Residence, Bella's Truck, Forks High, the hospital, etc. And La Push as well. Did some shopping in town, and especially loved talking to the people.

We're glad we stayed here — being the Cullen's house. The breakfasts were so good! We can't wait for another visit!

— Amanda + Jennifer Laguezzo
Brentwood, CA (Nor Cal)

We ♡ Twilight!
(especially Edward)

Note found in the Miller Tree Inn BB aka Cullen House guestbook, Forks, WA, USA.

as searching for fun and exciting experiences in the company of friends and/or family. Partying and meeting old friends are not highly ranked, which indicates that the friends a person is driven to share a travel experience with are primarily new people in the Twilight community.

Additionally, their lowest ranked reasons to travel indicate that the actual destination is of lesser importance. These results are supported by the answers to the question of whether the Twilight fans would have visited the destination they did on their most recent Twilight trip if it wasn't for Twilight, to which 65 per cent[XXI] answered that they wouldn't have.[17]

Based on their needs and desires, the tourists form an appreciation of the value of different companies' and organisations' offers. In general, customers value their use and experience of goods and services on the basis of what they get in return. As a tourist, for example, one gives time, money and energy to search for information about, buy and experience something.[18]

Value also influences the satisfaction that a tourist experiences: for example, the appreciation of quality and the extent to which one will repeat the behaviour and become a loyal customer. How value is appreciated depends on how much a product contributes to the customer fulfilling his/her needs or desires, and this appreciation can change over time. Additionally, value can be created at different levels; anything from an appreciated value based on what a place one visits looks like or its qualities, to the extent to which a trip corresponds to life's more overarching aims and values.

Customer-experienced value also varies depending on the situation and the type of person. There are also different types of value that complement each other.[19] For example, value can be divided into utility-based value, focusing on functional aspects such as financial value, convenience and efficiency, or hedonic-based value, which instead focuses on pleasure, entertainment, status and self-esteem. More specific types of value can be divided into performance/function, financial value/value for money, service value, social value, convenience and efficiency, emotional value, personal adaptation and relevance.[20]

Twilight tourists' highest ranked experienced value[21] on their most recent Twilight-related trip was *"I enjoyed the event/ trip"* ($\bar{x}$ =6.49), *"the event/trip made me feel good"* ($\bar{x}$=6.42), *"compared to other things I could have done, the time and effort spent*

[XXI] *n=694*

on this event/trip was truly enjoyable" ($\bar{x}$=6.39), *"the event/trip made me excited"* ($\bar{x}$=6.38) and *"the event/trip was well worth the time and effort spent"* ($\bar{x}$=6.26).[XXII]

To summarise, it can be said that these tourists experienced both utility-based values and more hedonic-based values during their trip. Emotionally charged types of value are always highly ranked, such as "the event/trip made me feel good and made me excited".[22]

Twilight tourists' future interest in travel

Perhaps the primary criticism that film and literature tourism faces is whether this form of tourism is long-term. This is because its main attraction is based on something as changeable as pop culture.[23] This is an important issue, not least when destinations have to consider investments in this form of tourism. One way to find the answer to this question is to ask the tourists themselves whether they plan to participate in similar trips in the future.

Out of the Twilight tourists[24], 64 per cent say that it is likely to extremely likely that they will participate in a future Twilight trip, of which 45 per cent say that it is extremely likely. Only 10 per cent say that it is not at all likely that they will take such a trip again.[XXIII]

Additionally, 61 per cent say that it is likely to extremely likely that they would recommend participation in a Twilight trip to others, of which 39 per cent say that it is extremely likely, while only 12 per cent believe that it is not likely at all.[XXIV] All of these results indicate long-term prospects for Twilight tourism based on the perspective of the travelling fans.[25]

[XXII] Scale 1–7 used, n=479–497
[XXIII] n=963
[XXIV] n=968

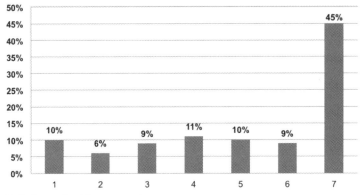

Twilight tourists' future travel.
(Scale: 1 = not likely at all, 7 = extremely likely)

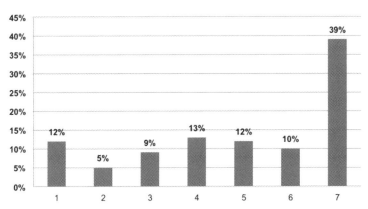

Twilight tourists' future travel recommendations.
(Scale: 1 = not likely at all, 7 = extremely likely)

References

[1] **International web survey** on "Twilight, tourism and social media" ETOUR Mid Sweden University. Contact: Christine Lundberg (Christine.Lundberg@miun.se)

[2] **International web survey** on "Twilight, tourism and social media" ETOUR Mid Sweden University. Contact: Christine Lundberg (Christine.Lundberg@miun.se)

[3] **http://twitarded.blogspot.com**/2011/09/forks-update-important-stuff-you-need.html

[4] **Swarbrook**, J. & Horner, S. (2006) *Consumer Behaviour in Tourism.* Butterworth Heinemann: Oxford.

[5] **Barnett**, M., & Standing, C. (2001) Repositioning Travel Agencies on the Internet. *Journal of Vacation Marketing, 7*(2), 143–152.
Buhalis, D. (1998) Strategic Use of Information Technologies in the Tourism Industry, *Tourism Management*, *23*(3), 207–220.
Mills, J. E., & Law, R. (2004). *Handbook of Consumer Behavior, Tourism, and the Internet*, The Haworth Hospitality Press. Binghamton: NY.
Xiang, Z., & Gretzel, U. (2010) Role of Social Media in Online Travel Information Search. *Tourism Management*, *31*(2), 179–188.

[6] **Frost**, W. (2006) *From Backlot to Runaway Production: Exploring Location and Authenticity in Film-Induced Tourism.* Working Paper Series ISSN 1327-5216 presented at the Second International Tourism and Media Conference in Melbourne, Monash University, Department of Management, Australia.

[7] **International web survey** on "Twilight, tourism and social media" ETOUR Mid Sweden University. Contact: Christine Lundberg (Christine.Lundberg@miun.se)

[8] **Crompton**, J. L. (1979) Motivations for Pleasure Vacation, *Annals of Tourism Research*, *6*(1), 408–424.
Dann, G. M. S. (1977) Anomi, Ego-Enhancement and Tourism, *Annals of Tourism Research*, *4*(4), 184–194.
Uysal, M., Gahan, L. & Martin, B. (1993) An Examination of Event Motivations. *Festival Management and Event Tourism*, *1*(1), 5–10.

[9] **Uysal**, M., Gahan, L. & Martin, B. (1993) An Examination of Event Motivations. *Festival Management and Event Tourism*, *1*(1), 5–10.

[10] **Smith**, A.C.T. & Stewart, B. (2007) The Travelling Fan: Understanding the Mechanisms of Sport Fan Consumption in a Sport Tourism Setting. *Journal of Sport & Tourism, 12*(3–4), 155–181 (p. 156).

[11] **Smith**, A.C.T. & Stewart, B. (2007) The Travelling Fan: Understanding the Mechanisms of Sport Fan Consumption in a Sport Tourism Setting. *Journal of Sport & Tourism, 12*(3–4), pp. 155–181 (p. 162).

[12] **Crawford**, G. (2004) *Consuming Sport: Fans, Sport and Culture*. Routledge: London.

Fink, J.S., Trail, G.S., & Anderson, D.F. (2002) An Examination of Team Identification: Which Motives are Most Salient to its Existence? *International Sports Journal*, Summer, 195–207.

Smith, A.C.T. & Stewart, B. (2007) The Travelling Fan: Understanding the Mechanisms of Sport Fan Consumption in a Sport Tourism Setting. *Journal of Sport & Tourism, 12*(3–4), 155–181.

Trail, G.T., & James, J.D. (2001) The Motivation Scale for Sport Consumption: Assessment of the Scale's Psychometric Properties. *Journal of Sport Behaviour*, *24*(1), 108–127.

Wann, D.L. (1995) Preliminary Validation of the Sport Fan Motivation Scale. *Journal of Sport and Social Issues*, *19*, 377–396.

Wann, D., Melnick, M., Russel, G., & Pease, D. (2001) *Sport fans: the Psychology and Social Impact of Spectators*. Routledge: New York.

Weed, M., & Bull, C. (2004) *Sports tourism: Participants, Policy and Providers*. Elsevier: Oxford.

[13] **Segrave**, J., & Chu, D. (1996) The Modern Olympic Games: An Access to Ontology. *Quest*, *48*, 57–66.

Smith, A.C.T. & Stewart, B. (2007) The Travelling Fan: Understanding the Mechanisms of Sport Fan Consumption in a Sport Tourism Setting. *Journal of Sport & Tourism, 12*(3–4), 155–181.

Trail, G.T., & James, J.D. (2001) The Motivation Scale for Sport Consumption: Assessment of the Scale's Psychometric Properties. *Journal of Sport Behaviour*, *24*(1), 108–127.

[14] **Morris**, D. (1981) *The Soccer Tribe*. Jonathan Cape: London.

Sutton, W.A., McDonald, M.A., Milne, G.R., & Cimperman, A.J. (1997) Creating and Fostering Fan Identification in Professional Sport. *Sport Marketing Quarterly*, *6*(1), 15–29.

Trail, G., Anderson, D.F., & Fink, J.S. (2000) A Theoretical Model of Sport Spectator Consumption Behavior. *International Journal of Sport Management*, *1*, 154–180.

[15] **Armstrong**, K.L. (2002) Race and Sport Consumption Motivations: A Preliminary Investigation of a Black Consumers' Sport Motivation Scale. *Journal of Sport Behavior*, *25*(4), 309–330.

Bilyeu, J.K., & Wann, D.L. (2002) An Investigation of Racial Differences in Sport Fan Motivation. *International Sports Journal*, *6*(2), 93–106.

James, J.D., & Ridinger, L.L. (2002) Female and Male Sport Fans: A Comparison of Sport Consumption Motives. *Journal of Sport Behavior*, *25*(3), 260–278.

Wann, D.L. (1995) Preliminary Validation of the Sport Fan Motivation Scale. *Journal of Sport and Social Issues*, *19*, 377–396.

[16] **International web survey** on "Twilight, tourism and social media" ETOUR Mid Sweden University. Contact: Christine Lundberg (Christine.Lundberg@ miun.se)

[17] **International web survey** on "Twilight, tourism and social media" ETOUR Mid Sweden University. Contact: Christine Lundberg (Christine.Lundberg@ miun.se)

[18] **Zeithmal**, V. A. (1988) Consumer Perceptions of Price, Quality, and Value: A Means-End Model Synthesis of Evidence. *Journal of Marketing*, *52*, 2–22.

[19] **Woodruff**, R. R., & Gardial, S. F. (1996) *Know Your Customers- New Approaches to Understanding Customer Value and Satisfaction*. Blackwell Publishing: Malden, USA.

Jagdish, S. N., Mittal B., & Newman, B. I. (1999) *Customer Behavior – Consumer Behavior and Beyond*. Thomson South-Western: Mason, USA.

[20] **Jagdish**, S. N., Mittal B., & Newman, B. I. (1999) *Customer Behavior – Consumer Behavior and Beyond*. Thomson South-Western: Mason, USA.

[21] **International web survey** on "Twilight, tourism and social media" ETOUR Mid Sweden University. Contact: Christine Lundberg (Christine.Lundberg@ miun.se)

[22]**International web survey** on "Twilight, tourism and social media" ETOUR Mid Sweden University. Contact: Christine Lundberg (Christine.Lundberg@ miun.se))

[23] **International web survey** on "Twilight, tourism and social media" ETOUR Mid Sweden University. Contact: Christine Lundberg (Christine.Lundberg@ miun.se)

[24] **International web survey** on "Twilight, tourism and social media" ETOUR Mid Sweden University. Contact: Christine Lundberg (Christine.Lundberg@ miun.se)

[25] **International web survey** on "Twilight, tourism and social media" ETOUR Mid Sweden University. Contact: Christine Lundberg (Christine.Lundberg@ miun.se)

Twilight fans on-line

"I just wanted to say that I love you gals. No, I really do. I can't believe that I found Twilight Mom's only three weeks ago! You all have given such warm welcomes, wonderful support, thought provoking conversation, and not to mention giving me the giggles and outright squeals. This is such a wonderful site, no crabbiness, all hugs. It gives me warm tingly feelings!/…/I feel the same way! I feel like I've joined a sorority of soul sisters who I just haven't met yet!"

TwiMoms on the significance of on-line communities.[1]

It is hardly surprising that fans of various phenomena express and share their interest with other fans on the Internet, for example through blogs and forums.[2] Perhaps what attract the fans are the characteristics of social media, in that they are interactive, dynamic and participant-focused.[3] From a tourism perspective, social media are increasingly important; for example, they are used for disseminating travel stories and evaluations, photos, travel planning and travel blogging.[4]

Research around the use of social media in tourism has primarily focused on how a destination or a company is presented in these media[5] and different perspectives on the effects of user behaviour.[6] A Few of the explanations for popularity of social media are that they are functional, social and exploratory. Additionally, they enable learning, research, relation building, creativity, entertainment and an escape from reality.[7]

Finding and sharing information about experiences, feeling a sense of belonging and a social identity, as well as entertainment, influences the degree of participation and attitudes to social media with tourism-based content.[8] For example, those who write about their travels on social media are sometimes driven by helping travel operators and consumers, their own pleasure and positive feedback from others.[9]

Numerous Internet sites, blogs, forums and on-line networks have been created by fans in order to share their common interest in Twilight. A Google search for "Twilight Saga" returned around 83,810,000 results and the search words "Twilight Saga blog" gave 343,000 results. Many of these include special interest blogs that fans create to blog about the stars. The biggest star is probably Robert Pattinson, who plays the vampire Edward Cullen. A search for his name generated around 40,300,000 results and "Robert Pattinson blog" gave around 64,200 hits. A search for his co-star, Kristen Stewart, who plays the young Bella Swan, generates around 32,400,000 results while "Kristen Stewart blog" gave around 61,800 hits. Another popular character is the werewolf Jacob Black. He is played by actor Taylor Lautner; a Google search on his name generated around 20,300,000 hits while the search words "Taylor Lautner blog" gave around 11,700 results.[10]

Another example of the fans' interest and involvement on the Internet is Summit Entertainment/Liongate's official Twilight page on Facebook; at the time of writing it has over 34 million fans.[11] 74 per cent of all Twilight fans visit a Twilight-related website, blog or forum every day or several times a day. 16 per cent visit them several times a week. Therefore, Twilight fans can be described as active Internet users.[12]

	% av n=1619
Several times a day	41%
Every day	33%
A few times a week	16%
Once every week	3%
A few times every month	3%
Once every month	1%
Less than every month	3%

Twilight fans visits to Twilight-related Internet sites.

On the Internet, fans discuss their own interpretation of the true meaning of Twilight's message, focusing on love, romance and desire:

> *"In both the virtual world and the real world, love, romance, and desire are held up as the meaning behind Twilight."*[13]

In addition, some fans, primarily older women, are dedicated to more superficial romantic content:

> *"albeit in a more "sexed-up" form/…/a sort of Playgirl for Twilight fans (sans the full-frontal nudity but with plenty of bare chests and bulging muscles)."*[14]

When Twilight fans look for Twilight-related information on the Internet, in our international Internet survey they say that their primary motives are "*to find information on the actors/ characters*", "*to find information in general*", "*to read or watch Twilight related content*" and "*to interact with other fans*".[1] As regards the fans' involvement through social media, they rank *"I'm interested in reading blogs about Twilight information and photos etc."*, *"when reading information in blogs I feel that the information is appealing"* and *"when reading information in blogs I feel that Twilight means a lot to me"* highest (see table below).[15]

---

[1] *n=794*

Social media involvement	Mean	n
I'm interested in reading blogs about Twilight information and photos etc.	6.12	906
When reading information in blogs I feel the information is appealing	5.65	893
When reading information in blogs I feel that Twilight means a lot to me	5.49	895
I think Twilight blogs provide good efficiency in information searching	5.39	892
I think Twilight blogs provide sufficient information	5.29	883
When reading information in blogs I feel that Twilight is relevant in my life	5.16	896
I think what is written in Twilight blogs is reliable	4.68	891
I think the communication in Twilight blogs is free from being interfered with by sales-persons	4.64	881
I think the communication in Twilight blogs is free from being interfered with by friends outside the Twilight community	4.61	882

Twilight fans' involvement with Twilight-related blogs.
(Scale: 1 = strongly disagree, 7 = strongly agree)

The Internet is important to Twilight fans who travel
Twilight fans also use blogs, websites and forums when they look for information and communicate before, during and after their Twilight travels. Many of them contain different forms of expressly tourist information (see below pictures) and other fans can search for and find travel information that may influence their travel behaviour. Twilight fandom can be described as very organised, not least with regards to travel. There are many trips that are organised by the fans themselves, for

example to places where the films were recorded or where the books are set, as well as to different types of events (e.g. Twi-MOMs conventions & get-togethers).[16]

The opening shots of the deer being hunted by vampires was shot at *Silver Falls State Park*, east of **Salem**, Oregon. Some of the tree climbing sequence was shot here as well. *"The Hunted"* also filmed extensively in this park.

Bella's house shown at the start of the film was at **22301 Cataro Dr.** in Santa Clarita, CA.

The large bridge that Charlie drives Bella over in the title sequence montage is the *Bridge of the Gods* over the Columbia River near **Stevenson, WA**.

The house where Charlie & Bella live in the film was shot at **184 S 6th St** in *St. Helens, OR*. They filmed the interiors here as well. Please beware it's on a dead-end private drive, so don't park here - walk. Enjoy it from the street & remember, people live here.

The greenhouses at *Clackamas Community College* were where Bella's science class had a field trip. This is located at **19600 Molalla Ave.** in Oregon City, OR. See the Google map below for the precise location.

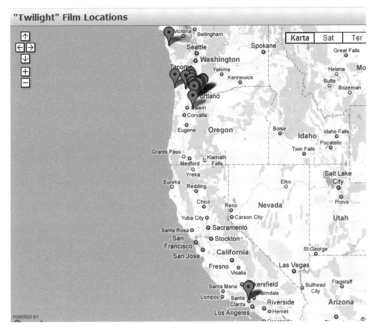

Place descriptions and a Google map created by fans, for filming sites for the first film in the Twilight series.[17]

Twilight fans make great use of information on the Internet when planning their trips. Also, the information on blogs and forums influences their decision to travel and during the trip itself. After the trip they share a great many of their travel experiences via social media (see below tables).[18]

Social media usage for travels	Mean	n
I have used information in blogs/communities to plan my participation	5.75	930
Information in blogs/communities was helpful while I participated	5.68	917
After I participated, I have shared my experiences on blogs/communities	5.42	922
Information in blogs/communities influenced my decision to participate	5.27	922
Information in blogs/communities influenced my decision NOT to participate	4.07	909

Twilight fans use of social media for travelling.
(Scale: 1= not at all, 7 = to a large extent).

These results show the significance of the Internet as a meeting place for fans who are interested in travelling to places associated with Twilight. It is also likely that fans who have not initially thought about travelling find inspiration in the stories and conversations about places which, when visited, can offer an extra emotionally charged relationship between these fans and Twilight.

References

[1] **www.twilightmoms.com** Forum: "So tell us why you love TwilightMOMS. com" Years: 2008–2011

[2] **Sandvoss**, C. (2005) *Fans*, Polity Press, UK

[3] **O'Reilly**, T. (2005) *What Is Web 2.0: Design Patterns and Business Models for the Next Generation of Software*. [Retrieved 15th of August 2011: http://www.oreillynet.com/pub/a/oreilly/tim/news/2005/09/30/what-is-web-20. html.]

[4] **Phocuswright**, (2010) *How Big is Social Media in Travel?*, FYI Newsletter [Received: 5th of April 2010]
Xiang, Z. & Gretzel, U. (2010) Role of Social Media in Online Travel Information Search, *Tourism Management, 31*, 179–188

[5] **Jeong**, E., & Jang, S. (2010) Restaurant Experiences Triggering Positive Electronic Word of Mouth (eWOM) Motivations. *International Journal of Hospitality Management, 30*(2), 356–366
Schmallegger, D., & Carson, D. (2009) Destination Image Projection on Consumer Generated Content Websites: A Case Study of the Flinders Ranges. *Information Technology & Tourism, 11*(2), 111–127
Wenger, A. (2008) Analysis of Travel Bloggers' Characteristics and Their Communication about Austria as a Tourism Destination. *Journal of Vacation Marketing, 14*(2), 169–176
Ye, Q, Law, R, & Gu, B. (2009) The Impact of Online User Reviews on Hotel Room Sales. *International Journal of Hospitality Management, 28*(1), 180–182
Zhang, Z., Ye, Qiang, Law, Rob, & Li, Y. (2010) The Impact of e Word of Mouth on the Online Popularity of Restaurants: A Comparison of Consumer Reviews and Editor Reviews. *International Journal of Hospitality Management, 29*(4), 694–700

[6] **Arsal**, I., Baldwin, E. D., & Backman, S. J. (2009) Member Reputation and its Influence on Travel Decisions: A Case Study of an Online Travel Community. *Information Technology & Tourism, 11*(3), 235–246
Casaló, L. V., Flavián, C. & Guinalíu, M. (2010) Determinants of the Intention to Participate in Firm Hosted Online Travel Communities and Effects on Consumer Behavioural intentions. *Tourism Management, 31* (6), 898–911
Huang, C.Y., Chou, C.J. & Lin, P.C. (2010) Involvement Theory in Constructing Bloggers' Intention to Purchase Travel Products. *Tourism Management, 31*, 513–526
Sanchez Franco, M. J., & Rondan Cataluña, F. J. (2010) Virtual Travel Communities and Customer Loyalty: Customer Purchase Involvement and Web Site Design. *Electronic Commerce Research and Applications, 9*(2), 171–182

[7] **Zhou**, Z., Jin, X-L., Vogel, D. R., Fang, Y. & Chen, X. (2011) Individual Motivations and Demographic Differences in Social Virtual World Uses: An Exploratory Investigation in Second Life, *International Journal of Electronic Commerce*, *31*, 261–271.

[8] **Chung,** J. Y., & Buhalis, D. (2008) Information Needs in Online Social Networks, *Information and Communication Technologies in Tourism, 10*, 267–281.
Casaló, L. V., Flavián, C. & Guinalíu, M. (2010) Determinants of the Intention to Participate in Firm Hosted Online Travel Communities and Effects on Consumer Behavioural Intentions. *Tourism Management*, *31*(6), 898–911.

[9] **Yoo**, K. H., & Gretzel, U. (2008) What Motivates Consumers to Write Online Travel Reviews? *Information Technology & Tourism*, *10*(4), 283–295.

[10] **Google search** [18th of April 2010]

[11] **https://www.facebook.com**/#!/twilight [Retrieved: 26th of June 2012]

[12] **International web survey** on "Twilight, tourism and social media" ETOUR Mid Sweden University. Contact: Christine Lundberg (Christine.Lundberg@ miun.se)

[13] **Wilson**, N. (2011) *Seduced by Twilight: The Allure and Contradictory Messages of the Popular Saga,* McFarland & Company Inc: Jefferson, US, p. 44.

[14] **Wilson**, N. (2011) *Seduced by Twilight: The Allure and Contradictory Messages of the Popular Saga,* McFarland & Company Inc: Jefferson, US, p. 44.

[15] **International web survey** on "Twilight, tourism and social media" ETOUR Mid Sweden University. Contact: Christine Lundberg (Christine.Lundberg@ miun.se)

[16] **http://twitarded.blogspot.com**/2011/09/forks-update-important-stuff-you-need.html
http://sites.google.com/site/wafilmlocations/filmsblog/twilight2008
www.twilightmoms.com

[17] **http://sites.google.com**/site/wafilmlocations/filmsblog/twilight2008

[18] **International web survey** on "Twilight, tourism and social media" ETOUR Mid Sweden University. Contact: Christine Lundberg (Christine.Lundberg@ miun.se)

Destination Twilight

"Well this crazy thing that happened to us in this little tiny town is a huge gift and we are extremely fortunate and it has done us a world of good."

Staff at the visitor center in Forks on Twilight and Twilight tourism

In order to achieve a deeper understanding of Twilight tourists' travels, it is important to understand the places – destinations – to which they travel. These places are, as previously discussed, *settings* (where the events occur) or *locations* (where the films are recorded).[1]

One proposed definition of a destination is that it is a place where there is a combination of available products and services that may attract visitors.[2] Quality and perceived value are basic values of the destination and for the tourist; however, these experiences are by nature complex. It may sometimes be difficult for a destination to know what produces a feeling of quality and value in a tourist and how these feelings are experienced. There is often a link between a destination's products and how they are experienced.[3]

In the case of Twilight, the most important *setting-destinations* are two small communities in the USA and one in Italy – Forks and La Push in Washington and Volterra in Tuscany. The most important *location-destinations* are British Columbia in Canada and Montepulciano in Italy. In addition to these destinations, official and unofficial Twilight events and conventions are organised several times a year in large cities around the world, attracting thousands of visitors.

This chapter deals with three settings – Forks, La Push and Volterra – and two locations – British Columbia and Montepulciano.

Twilight destinationer		Other destinations
Settings	*Locations*	*Examples of events and conventions*
Forks and La Push, Washington, USA	British Columbia, Canada	Twicon in the USA Eternal Twilight in Great Britain
Volterra, Italy Italy	Montepulciano, Indonesia	Fan events – e.g. in Indonesia Marketing events – e.g. in South Korea

Overview of Twilight-related destinations.

Forks and La Push, WA, USA
– Home of vampires and werewolves

Forks is a small town in Clallam County, Washington, USA, with 3,532 inhabitants.[4] Historically, Forks has lived off the timber industry, but has also long been a popular destination for fishermen and visitors to the national park. However, tourism increased enormously after Stephenie Meyer released the first book in the Twilight Saga.[5] The town of Forks is where the majority of the action in Twilight takes place.

La Push is also a small community in Clallam County, USA, with 371 inhabitants, only seven and half kilometres from Forks.[6] This is the community in which the Native American Quileute people have their home, which is also portrayed in Twilight. The Quileute people have always been spiritual, although after the arrival of the Europeans, a great deal of their original religion was lost. According to their traditions, each person has a spirit guide and they prayed together with the sun and the universe to keep it. Quileute legends describe how their people are descended from wolves. According to the myth, two characters were responsible for creating the first person in the Quileute, known as Alpha, by transforming a wolf. Stephenie Meyer's depiction of the people in Twilight is fictionalised, where she recounts the legend of how the Quileutes are descended from wolves and how the contemporary Quileute people can shape-shift into wolves/werewolves, who are enemies of the vampires.[7]

La Push has recently become known for its surfing, whale watching, hiking and fishing, and now for its portrayal in Twilight.[8]

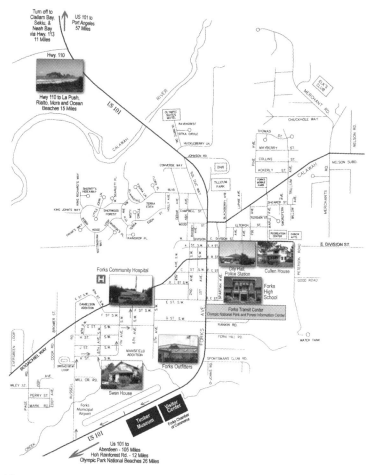

Map of Forks with important places from Twilight marked. Published with the permission of the Forks Visitor Center.

Vampire warning sign on the border between La Push and Forks.

In Forks, a representative from the visitor center recounts what happened when the first Twilight tourists arrived in 2005 and said: *"We are here because of a book we read"*. This reason to travel was completely unknown to the visitor center staff at that time: *"This was nothing we prepared for"*. They say that they couldn't in their wildest dreams have imagined Forks would be involved in anything like the pop culture phenomenon that is Twilight. In the start-up phase, the visitor center didn't feel supported by the rest of the town, as no one believed that the Twilight phenomenon would get as big as it has, so they felt that it was their responsibility to develop a product that the Twilight tourists could consume.

Twilight tourism started in Forks in 2005, and they now have up to 500 Twilight visitors to the tourist office every day:

> *"2007 it jumped from 6,000 people to 10,000 people and it's really jumped in 2008 because the first movie came out."*

The staff at the visitor center and the town's mayor talk about the major adjustments that Twilight tourism has entailed:

> *"People kept coming in larger and larger groups, and every day we were just going: 'we cannot believe this!*

Oh my God! These are just fictional'…and we still have the same attitude. We can still not believe this is actually happening to us in Forks. And we are tickled! We are very pleased! We keep pinching each other all the time, and this has been going on for years/…/could never in our wildest imagination believe we would be involved in anything like this/…/who ever thought it was going to be this big!"

Infrastructure in places that previously did not attract many tourists may be problematic as it is not suitable for the demands of increased tourism; the infrastructure is often built to cope with existing demand, not to cope with increased demand. Other users of these services, such as local residents, often develop a negative attitude to tourism when the infrastructure doesn't have enough capacity to handle increased tourist flows.[9]

Infrastructure in Forks, such as accommodation, has not had particular problems due to increased tourist flows. However, the visitor center has individual examples of dissatisfied local residents who have suddenly had to wait at road junctions, which was never the case before, due to increased traffic.

Six factors have been described as components of a destination's macro environment; the economic, demographic, natural, political, technological and cultural factors that influence the visitor's experience and perception of a destination.[10] Social factors also shape the macro environment. The friendliness of the locals, the language that is spoken and population density are attributes that contribute to the macro environment. Culture is another important factor that creates many tourism experiences.[11]

Managers at the visitor center in Forks say that more jobs have been created after the arrival of an entirely new industry, locally called the Twilight industry, to which they consider the town has a positive attitude. They also receive large amounts of emails from Twilight fans asking about jobs available in the region, and who are considering settling in Forks despite never having visited it before! In Forks, practically all businesses have been affected by Stephenie Meyer's choice of the town as the site of the action in her books. This has resulted in there now being many more opportunities for both residents and tourists, with a wider range of shops and other businesses.

An increased touristic demand may be experienced as something positive by the local population, giving better quality of life, for example. Others may be of the opposite opinion and see this industry and increased touristic demand as something negative, which may mean that residents lose their integrity and their character.[12] In Forks, the visitor center staff say that they are proud of Forks and that the town's inhabitants have welcomed Twilight and the Twilight tourists, almost without exception. Only the town's teenagers were openly negative at the start of Twilight tourism's development; they were discontented about the numbers of tourists who visited their school to take photographs and who sometimes behaved rudely. Staff at the visitor center say:

> *"I think the whole town looked at them and: Hello kids, grow up, this is a good thing for us/…/We want to stay alive and this has been an industry that expanded everything to our benefit. So not all are happy, but 98% are happy."*

An author in Forks recounts talking to some members of the Quileute people in La Push, who stated that they regard the films as comedies, as they don't reflect their true everyday life! Despite this, he says they feel some pride at being associated with Twilight.

Researchers in tourism increasingly believe that more cooperation between the various stakeholders at a destination should be initiated in the planning process. It is suggested that the most basic element of this process is the need to involve the people or groups who are directly affected by the planning and the resulting developments. Additionally, Sautter and Leisen (1998) say that cooperation between key stakeholders is essential in achieving sustainable development.[13] Freeman (1984) proposes that a destination is characterised by relationships between a number of groups and individuals, from employees, customers and suppliers to different public authorities with different interests and needs.[14] This definition includes a very broad cross-section; other definitions are more limited, with only those who are directly financially affected being regarded as stakeholders.[15]

Managers at the visitor center in Forks describe how they have experienced challenges in the relationship between Forks and La Push, and how Twilight has brought this to a head:

> "Our relationship with the Quileute tribe has always been a little different. They do not answer to the same things as we do so we kind of danced around each other, seeing how we fit together with this story. It is their story, but it is also our story and we have cast people to go over their reservation and we distribute etiquette lists so the people don't offend them. We wanna make sure they remain happy. So it has been a challenge."

Forks' mayor says that Forks and the Quileute people in La Push regard each other as one community, but that it hasn't always been that way. However, he adds that cooperation between Forks and La Push relating to Twilight tourism has been successful:

> "I would like to say that we think of ourselves like one community, but that is not always the case, and sometimes there are issues between us. La Push and the Qui-

leute have been absolutely wonderful through all of this, they are just great/.../They brought in a tourism coordinator and we always know they are going to do things the way they want it, that works for them, and that is something that I know, I respect, and I think that most of the locals' respect. When the day is done, we are all doing this together."

Forks' mayor says that there were a number of problems for La Push and the Quileute people, after they were portrayed in Twilight, due to the resulting tourism. These have included historic sites and holy burial grounds not being treated with respect. He provides an example of one such event:

"They have some difficulties with people coming in from the outside, disrespecting their culture and their heritage. They also have some issues with the tour companies going down there, I do not know if the tour companies going all the way down there but they wanted money from the tour companies running on the reservation, which is as far as I'm concerned, absolutely within their right. But other than that, it has been pretty good/.../the biggest issue they had was a TV-crew that was down there filming the graveyard which was just an absolute no no."

One consequence of the disrespect of the Quileute's heritage was that they hired a PR consultant from JTalentgroup in Seattle. This is an organisation for indigenous Americans, which developed restrictions for visitors. The chairman of Quileute Nation says that it was important for them to work with an organisation they can identify with and which respects their core values – protecting their culture and respecting their land – but which also understands that they also welcome people from the entire world.[16] The founder and representative of JTalentgroup says the following about helping the Quileute tribe to create sustainable tourism:

> *"I am honored to work with the Quileute Nation/.../ to assisting them with sharing their cultural identity and heritage with the world. The Twilight Saga has put them in the international spotlight and afforded them the opportunity to share their own stories, dances, food and other traditions passed down from generation to generation."*[17]

Films have an active role in people's social constructions and can thus be an important tool in marketing a destination.[18] The staff at Forks visitor center confirm this:

> *"Even [when placing] orders for gifts for Christmas, where you say where you live in Forks, it is an immediate reaction, it's fabulous! It is just an incredible gift."*

A large part of cooperative destination marketing and product development takes place on an ad hoc basis through tourism operators, such as local restaurants and hotels.[19] This has also been the case in Forks. As regards product development, Forks visitor center states that when the Twilight tourists started to arrive, there was no cooperation or joint strategy in the town:

> *"No one really thought this was going to be big. It was just on us, 'let's make something for them to do'. We kind of started it up."*

A study by Hudson and Ritchie showed that a majority of the local population on the Greek island of Cephalonia were pleased that the production company removed the sets after a film was recorded there. They wanted to preserve their island as it was before the filming and without any resulting mass tourism.[20] This is a noticeable difference to Forks, where people are grateful for the attention they have received due to Twilight, and which they have themselves created staged environments for. The physical environment in which the tourism experience takes place, called the *servicescape* or *experiencescape*, has an important role in the visitors' impressions of the place that is being visited.[21] The servicescape is also of great importance for the visitor's first impression, as this comprises the physical environment that is experienced before any human interaction has time to take place[22] and is vital in creating excitement.[23] These environments are also significant for travel linked to pop culture tourism phenomena, such as film and literature tourism. Below are a number of examples of product development in Forks' Twilight environments.

One of the town's bed and breakfasts, the *Cullen House*, was selected by the visitor center to represent an important place in bringing the book's events to life for the fans, as it is the house in which the Twilight characters in the Cullen family live. The owners remember when the first Twilight tourists arrived in 2005 and surprisingly started asking for places that were described in the book:

> *"We had a father and daughter coming from Arizona to stay with us and the girl asked; 'where is Forks High School and how do we find the hospital'? And just asked different questions and I was not familiar with the book."*

Since then, Cullen House has become a Twilight-themed accommodation (with rooms decorated with Twilight books and films, "personal family photos" of the Cullen family, themed signs and a letterbox for the Cullens) and the owners talk about their latest product investment, which is a newly decorated room:

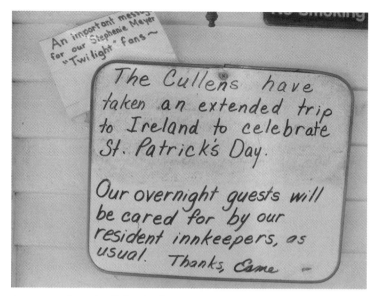

An important message for our Stephenie Meyer "Twilight" fans ~

The Cullens have taken an extended trip to Ireland to celebrate St. Patrick's Day.

Our overnight guests will be cared for by our resident innkeepers, as usual. Thanks, Came

A message from the Cullen family to tourists on the front door to Miller Tree Inn B&B, also known as Cullen House.

"We have just about completed the room that we are calling 'Carlisle's Office' and hope to bring visitors in to see it within the next couple of weeks."

The mayor of Forks confirms the image that visitor center gives, of how no one saw the potential in developing products for Twilight tourists in the immediate start-up phase. He believes that the caution was explained by residents not believing that it was sustainable in the long-term. However, it was a Twilight fan from Vancouver, WA, who realised the lack of souvenir products during her visit to the town. She then moved to Forks and opened the *Dazzled by Twilight* souvenir shop. The mayor also explains how a florist's changed its concept to meet increased demand:

"The Lapells picked up on it pretty quickly, it just started coming so many tourists in there looking for something

to do, and they were probably the first family to pick it up/.../I think the locals wanted to be really cautious because I did not think that anybody wanted to change their business form to find that this lasted for a year and all suddenly they lost their local, or what they did."

After this, according to both the mayor and the visitor center staff, more local stakeholders adapted their offer to the demands of the Twilight tourists:

"After that time, I think that the pharmacy got Twilight [things] in there and Forks Outfitters and it showed up all along down town. [A restaurant included] Twilight themed things on the restaurant menus. He came up with the Bella Burger/.../already two years ago he made 25,000 of them/.../you can go and have a Bella Burger, you can get Bellasagnia, with Ed Bread and Swan Salad."

After the first hamburger was put on the menu, increasing numbers of restaurants introduced themed menus and there was more themed accommodation:

"We started to see value added motel rooms, we started seeing signs around the town, the doctor Cullen parking

place up at the hospital, the Chamber went around to pick the Swan House/…/because they [the tourists] did not care whether the movie was filmed here or not, they were still coming here."

Forks visitor center also produced a map of Forks showing important places from the books, such as the police station and the Swan's and the Cullen's houses, which has been a hit:

"We thought, well we need as much information if not more information than Twilight fans so that we can satisfy them and play along with them and tell them stories/…/We know it was successful because people felt they were a part of this. They could actually come to a place which was named in the book and we could actually put them in contact with the places named in the book. So it began there and it was such a success."

Since 2007, Forks has held an annual event to honour the author Stephenie Meyer and what she has done for the town. It is called *Stephenie Meyer Day* and is held on the birthday of the character of Bella, 13 September. In the first year the event was held, it attracted 908 fans. In subsequent years this increased to 1500 and then to 2000 visitors. A representative of the visitor center says that Twilight tourists book a year in advance, and

Parking place outside Forks hospital for the Twilight character Dr Carlisle Cullen.

Twilight-related sign in the window of the local printers.

The Cullen family's letter box outside the Miller Tree Inn B&B, also known as Cullen House.

that many of them must stay a long way from Forks during the event due to the lack of accommodation. Activities include a range of competitions, such as best costume, best decorated card and group photos:

> *"It has become a real happening in Forks, it's become a phenomenal success."*

The mayor of Forks also talks about one piece of product development that wasn't a success. This concerned a young man who was very similar to one of the main characters in the film, Edward Cullen. This man offered Twilight tourists a photo taken with him, for a set price. The mayor believes that his failure was due to coming from a city and being unable to adapt to small town life in Forks.

One unexplored product development is considered, by the visitor center in Forks, to be the crafts that are made by the residents of La Push. However, they are not interested in developing this even if the demand is there, which the visitor center explains with the fact that it is not part of their culture.

The physical elements of a destination may include a place or building, natural resources such as scenic areas, flora and fauna, and also physical conditions such as the weather.[24] Forks is characterised by its grey and rainy weather. It was this characteristic that led Stephenie Meyer to choose to locate the action in Forks. To find the perfect place for her story, she looked for the place in the US that had the most precipitation, as vampires are sensitive to sunlight. This turned out to be on the Olympic Peninsula in the state of Washington. Her own description of the place she was looking for is:

"[I needed] someplace ridiculously rainy."

When she discovered Forks, she also found its neighbour La Push and the reserve on which the Quileute Nation has its home. She found the tribe's history so fascinating that she chose to put some fictional members of the tribe in her story.[25]

Managers at the visitor center in Forks describe how Twilight tourists arrive on sunny days and question the weather conditions:

*"People expect it to be rainy; they can be disappointed if
the sun is shining/…/Because when you read the books,
Bella talks about the raining all the time, so people have
the expectations that it rains every single day of the year
here/…/so when people come here in the summer and
it's not rainy, people are very disappointed so we have
to apologize."*

One of the visitor center's representatives expresses fascination
over the author's way of capturing the authentic environments
in her writing:

*"She has an incredible imagination and she captures it
and they [the tourists] come here to see if it really looks
like that and miraculously it does."*

As described above, many of the tourism servicescapes in Forks
are themed and staged, and thus adapted to Twilight tourists.
However, there are also examples of natural landscapes; one
example of a natural servicescape is the coastline near to La
Push, which is not artificial and which is a popular destination
for Twilight tourists.

Perceptions of genuineness in tourism experiences are usually summarised using the concept of authenticity. This term
was introduced in studies of tourists' motivations, activities
and experiences by MacCannell[26] and has been defined as a
belief that something is real and reliable.[27] The term authenticity has made critics question its viability within tourism, as
they feel that tourists' motivations and experiences cannot be
explained by this, and it thus has limited use.[28] Regarding the
issue of authenticity in film, it is not just about the film por-
traying facts correctly, but also about the filmmaker's own interpretations and the actors' motivation.[29]

Authenticity is an important concept in film and literature
tourism, but it is open to question how authentic a film or

literature tourism experience can be, as they are often about fictional places' attractions. In many cases, reality is mixed with fiction.[30] Hudson and Ritchie suggest that the destinations that are most successful after being portrayed in a film are ones that were portrayed with an authentic image, and where the film has succeeded in capturing the nature of the place. This is true regardless of whether it applies to the landscape or the cultural content. The tourist's perception of the experience's authenticity is an interplay between the phenomena, the place and the tourist's interaction with them.

One of the problems that may occur is that the film tourist's image of the place is not equivalent to the experience of the place when it is visited, which may result in disappointment.[31] Another aspect of this is what Frost calls *local dissonance,* meaning the effect that may occur due to the difference between where the film was recorded and where the events in it occured.[32] Managers at the visitor center in Forks have thought a lot about whether Twilight tourists would choose to visit Forks or not, as none of the films were recorded at the destination:

> *"We were actually wondering about it, when they decided to film elsewhere, how many people will come to Forks? We then discovered that most people still want to come to Forks because it is the real Forks from the stories."*

The staff at Forks visitor center feels a little overlooked due to the films not being recorded in Forks, as they meet the tourists' need for authenticity through their work. However, they estimate that the figure is only ten per cent, and that the remaining ninety per cent know the films were not recorded in Forks:

> *"We are a little bit offended they didn't film anything here. On the other hand, we benefit it, but still, people come here and sometimes they are angry because the movie was not made here."*

View of a beach close to La Push.

Authenticity in film meets authenticity in literature: Bella's cars (the model described in the book and the one from the film) outside Forks Visitor Center.

It can be claimed that the authenticity of the tourist experiences in La Push is strengthened by the author's depiction of the Quileute tribe's legends, history and culture in the books.[33] This means that the impression of authenticity is more entwined with the experience than it is for an entirely fictional place and/or story.

Volterra, Italy – stronghold of the Volturi vampire clan

Volterra is a town with 11,100 inhabitants, situated in Tuscany, Italy, around 60 kilometres south-east of Pisa. Volterra has a mediaeval centre and the town is a manufacturing centre for alabaster crafts. Its industry is mainly mining (copper, salt and alabaster), but it also has a growing tourist industry.[34] As with Forks, Twilight tourism came as a complete surprise to the town, according to the staff at the tourist office in Volterra. A tourist office representative talks about the starting point, which was the author Stephenie Meyer's visit to the town in 2007, for the launch of the second book in the series – New Moon:

> *"So she came in 2007/…/ and presented her book/…/ the Italian version/…/so they filled up the theatre, and Stephenie Meyer, she did her reading here as well at the theatre in Volterra, the theatre was full…and we couldn't imagine that, actually. Only then we got to know that 'wow, it's big, it has to be a big thing'/…/ And we were actually not prepared to have lots of buses coming to see her, so we were not aware at all of this project."*

After that, Twilight tourism dropped off slightly, but rebounded when the first film in the series was released:

> *"November 2008, when the first movie, Twilight, came out and when Summit Entertainment decided to also*

do the second movie, and then it really started. 'Cause then, from November on... I remember we had our office closed for two days because we were out on a business trip all, and we came back/.../and we had our mailbox full of requests [with] 'when are they coming to shoot the movie?' and so on/.../now it is like, a hundred times a day, for a minimum."

At the tourist office in Volterra, the staff members are critical of their own actions when decision-time came for which Italian city the series' second film would be filmed in. A decision that meant the neighbouring town of Montepulciano was chosen for filming instead of Volterra:

"Maybe we were a bit self-confident, too self-confident, and we thought well, either they come... if they come to Italy and shoot it, they will come to Volterra."

When it was realised that the town was not a natural recording site for the film, Volterra offered the film production company financial compensation and full service during their stay in Italy, as compensation for the company locating filming in their town:

"We did everything. So first we started to write letters to them/.../and at the end we offered quite some remuneration, we also offered them total hospitality here in Volterra, which means for the whole staff accommodation as well as catering... for...it was worth like 500,000 Euros, but it wasn't enough/.../we were very very disappointed/.../We are having lots of trouble now, people coming to Volterra and they think that it has been shot here in Volterra and it hasn't, so they get really disappointed."

For Volterra, as with Forks, this caused a problem with *local dissonance*.[35] However, at the tourist office in Volterra, they believe that the fans travel to both Volterra and Montepulciano, despite there sometimes being different expectations and perceptions of which destination is associated with the books and the films:

> *"Who is really a Twilighter goes to both places, they come here and they go to Montepulciano. There are also quite a number of persons who like the books and the movies not, who… you say it wasn't shot here, and they say 'well, I don't care, because I am a fan of the book'. We can be happy with the numbers; the people still come to Volterra."*

Increased pressure on infrastructure due to increased touristic demand may, as previously mentioned, cause problems.[36] In Volterra, the capacity has been just adequate for overnight accommodation. At peak season it is fully booked from May to September, but that was also the case before Twilight tourists started flooding to the town. Volterra has many day trippers, which means that the issue of accommodation has not yet been a problem for the town.

Increased load on the infrastructure can also result in negative attitudes towards tourism from the local population.[37] A representative of the tourist office in Volterra says that only a few local residents have displayed negative reactions to Twilight tourism, and they have been related to tourists finding it difficult to differentiate between Volterra and Montepulciano. In general, the local population have been positive about the phenomenon:

> *"I think that in the end everybody are having a profit out of it/…/I think in the end, everybody is happy about everything."*

Collins and Doorley have proposed four significant constituents to an alliance. These are shared dependence, cooperation, effect on a competitive position and life-long relations.[38] A strategic alliance, based on Collins and Doorley's reasoning, is cooperation between two or more organisations over a given time period, with the aim of winning competitive advantage. These varying alliances and partnerships can be entirely different. Some may have clearly defined aims and clear relationships between the members, while others represent a hidden understanding between the members, in which aims and relationships are not formally declared or specified.

Cooperation and alliances between the private and public sectors are particularly important in destination marketing. This is because there is often a correlation between the aims of both sectors – to attract more tourists to the destination. This can also boost the social targets of the public sector. Stakeholders may, despite the potential benefits that the tourism destination's marketing alliances have, perceive a low potential for tourism's development and thus not see the benefits of investing in an alliance. The stakeholders that are located in attractive areas may feel that it is not necessary to have further cooperation to attract visitors.[39]

The staff members at the tourist office in Volterra say that when demand began for Twilight products, they realised that they needed to work with stakeholders in the town; they invited them for an initial meeting:

> *"We invited different stakeholders, hotels, restaurants/…/ tried to involve as many people as possible/…/our webmaster as well and we decided on a project and sure, we could have done much better."*

Volterra makes some use of Twilight to help Twilight tourists discover Volterra's historical background when they have arrived in the town. They feel that Stephenie Meyer has helped with this, as her books describe the royal vampire clan of the Volturi (which rule the town according to Twilight) as being ancestors to the Etruscans. As regards the destination's authenticity, which in this case is linked to how well the author captures the characteristics of the destination[40], the author's link between the fictional (Volturi) and the town's own history (Etruscans) means that its authenticity is boosted. They work actively to maintain their own cultural identity:

> *"We have to deal with it [Twilight tourism], and we want to deal with it in the best sustainable way. So we don't want to become the city of the vampires. That is very very important for us."*

However, many shops sell some Twilight products, such as T-shirts depicting the characters' faces, but some have also made their own creations to sell to fans. One example is bowls that are decorated with a flower inspired by the books' covers and made from alabaster, for which Volterra is traditionally famous. They are critical of products that they perceive as having a more commercial focus, such as Montepulciano's vampire wine:

> *"We did something because we had to, and that's fun about this, but honestly spoken, what Montepulciano did to make their wine which is famous all over the world, and they made the Volturi wine out of it, is something that we, honestly spoken, didn't like a lot. It's like, you know, I can't put a wine that is that important, the Rosso di Montepulciano, sell it for vampires, it's something that is not our…our philosophy/…/we want to value our territory we have, and that's more important than vampires."*

Volterra's most famous landmark for Twilight tourists – the clock tower.

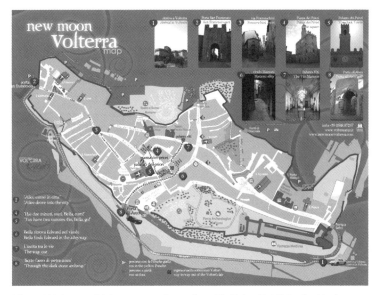

Map of Volterra with important places from Twilight. Published with the permission of Volterra's tourist office.

As previously mentioned, the servicescape is important to visitors and their impression of the destination. The physical
elements of a destination, such as a place or building, can be
significant servicescapes.[41] In Volterra, the town's clock tower
is the most distinctive landmark for the Twilight tourists. The
clock tower is described in the New Moon book and shown in
the film of the same name (though this was the clock tower in
Montepulciano, where the film was recorded), in association
with a very dramatic event. Unlike Forks, Volterra does not
have staged Twilight servicescapes.

   In the work to satisfy the needs of Twilight tourists, Volterra's tourist office has developed a map that shows Twilight-
related locations in the town. Their primary product for visiting fans is a guided Twilight tour, which is sometimes more
than fully-booked:

"We show to the tourists the typical place of Volterra with Volturi saga."

They also receive many special requests from Twilight tourists for guided tours, and try to fulfil these as well as they can. The tourist office has also arranged "reunions" for New Moon fans, but experience difficulties in meeting this demand. This is because Volterra has become so much more attractive as a destination for Twilight tourists, while the tourist office's staffing has not increased at the same rate as demand. The town now works in a more planned manner with the development and management of Twilight tourism, which is still extensive, although declining slightly:

"We try to control, to plan this phenomenon/.../Twilight tourists are still invading the city, although of course numbers are dropping now, but we have been prepared for that."

British Columbia, Canada – a stage for film vampires and werewolves

British Columbia is a Canadian province with 4.3 million inhabitants. It is mountainous and richly forested, with the Rocky Mountains covering much of its area. The majority of the population lives in and around Vancouver, which has 2 million inhabitants. Vancouver is Canada's third city and has an important port. It also has a major international airport and is the terminus of the transcontinental railways. The base of its economy is trade and transport. In addition to timber, foodstuffs, metal and machine industries, tourism is an important source of income. Vancouver hosted the Winter Olympics in 2010.[42]

British Columbia is the third largest production centre in the world for film and television, behind Los Angeles and New York City, and has thus been named "Hollywood North". The epithet probably means the whole of Canada's film and television production, but primarily that of British Columbia and Vancouver, which is the centre for the majority of its production[43], including four of five Twilight films. A representative of British Columbia's Film Commission states that the region is known for being a very attractive production centre:

> "Vancover/British Columbia is seen as being extremely attractive as a production center, it's full service, we have from pre-production right through the post, and all the capabilities and services in between."

The costs associated with making a film are often given as a reason why films are recorded in a country other than the one where the events take place. The high cost of recording a film in the US, for example, results in film production companies locating filming abroad. The usual incentives are lower payroll costs, lower costs for using places as locations and the availability of state subsidies. A significant contributing factor for productions – particularly foreign productions – choosing British Columbia as a location has been the tax relief on offer. Their tax system has been strategically planned to attract this type of industry to their region. A representative of the British Columbia Film Commission explains why so many film productions are located in British Columbia, emphasising the tax and service systems:

> "It is an industry that we are dependent on service workers to a large degree and there are so many variables in that! – Which we have no control of. Whether there is the Canadian dollar, or the tax credits and other jurisdictions. That is the other probably large drawing factor for British Columbia, the fact that we have very good tax credits. That has been since 1998, what has helped to draw activity here, especially foreign activity."

Another advantage for Vancouver and British Columbia as a film production region is, according to the representative of the British Columbia Film Commission, that the city has good flight links with Los Angeles. It also has good infrastructure in the form of studios and specially-built studios:

> *"We also in the ten last years developed a centre of visual effects so that there is a number of very successful award winning visual effects and post-production companies that has developed as the industry has grown here. Then we've also seen a numbers of companies that have come to British Columbia that are American based or whatever, because there is that level of production activity here/…/Rather than be in LA they will set up an office in Vancouver, we have large international companies. That is a whole other aspect of the industry that has helped us because you do not have to send it out anywhere else, you can do it all the way through here."*

The phenomenon of locations that are places other than those where the events in the film take place, is called *runaway productions* by Croy and Walker.[44] The concept of *local dissonance* is linked to this. Frost describes this using the film Braveheart (1995) as an example; this was mostly filmed in Eire, but is about the Scottish patriot William Wallace and the events take place in Scotland. The choice of Eire as a location was primarily due to lower production costs and free use of a large number of extras.[45]

The lack of cooperation between creative industries (e.g. film, television, literature) and the tourist industry has been described in the literature.[46] This is confirmed by a tour operator in Vancouver who runs a guide company, guiding tourists to various locations for film and television series, including the Twilight films. She believes that the production companies do not realise the value of increased tourism flows to the region:

"I don't think they understand that at all. I think that they are very narrowed-minded. I think that they only see their own profit."

She also believes that the production companies use Vancouver for what they need during filming and that they are not interested in any spin-off business. Another reason for the lack of cooperation between the industries is due to the production companies' need to protect their products:

"All they see is if people are looking at their production, they ruin the surprise at the box office, like you can only look at my production if you pay money to sit in the

British Columbia Film Commission

British Columbia Film Commission was established in 1978 and aims to attract both local and international filmmakers to the region, to market British Columbia's scenery and to offer locations and service (transport, catering, specially-built studios, and so on, and the manpower needed to service a project). They have their own staff with the capacity to work on 40 productions in parallel. The only things a production company need to bring to the region are the producers and directors. They describe their task in the following way: *"Both to attract them here and once they are here, to make sure they have a successful production experience. We facilitate relationships in the industry and specific access to locations/.../we have over 200 productions a year, films, TV series, documentaries. 70–80 % done in British Columbia is US financed"*.

seat when it is finished, but don't look at it before it is finished."

A representative from Tourism Vancouver describes the same thing, but from the production company's perspective, where the aim is not to attract attention from inquisitive tourists and the general public during filming:

> *"The film producers/.../they are coming to a community, they do what they need to do and they will disappear completely unnoticed from the community. The last thing they want is to have a lot of attention/.../they try to keep it very discrete."*

The tour operator in Vancouver says that she and her customers face a negative attitude from representatives from the film production companies during her guided tours, which can lead to dissatisfaction among her customers:

> *"It is more; let's see how dumb they can behave, how rude...When actually they are supposed to be very nice and polite and they are not."*

One explanation for this behaviour, offered by a representative of British Columbia's Film Commission, is the security that surrounds filming. Many of the places that are used as locations are on private ground and there are confidential contracts that must be respected:

> *"They are our clients and we respect the confidentiality, that's why also they come here."*

She also says that the film production companies do not benefit from cooperating with the tourism industry:

"They spend millions of dollars on marketing budgets. And they are not from here, so it's difficult how to know how to capitalize on the potential opportunity that film tourism can provide."

Despite these difficulties in balancing security issues in the film industry and tourism, the representative from the British Columbia Film Commission says that there is hope for cooperation between them. She also says that there is a grey zone between the industries and that the tourist industry does not know how to use the opportunities for developing film tourism:

"I think it comes down to cross benefits because our visitors are actually going to British Columbia because they are interested in a particular film/…/the tourism people do not know the best way to capitalize and they don't know what opportunities, and to make those opportunities materialized I guess…because we are saying to them aah, you can't do that…"

Tour operator in Vancouver

The company started business in 2008 and provides guided tours to locations used in film and television series in British Columbia. The entrepreneur has a background in business development and communication and describes herself as a photojournalist, as she also takes photographs of actors that visit the region and distributes these on the Internet.

Additionally, the British Columbia Film Commission says that its commission is film production and that the tourist industry is outside its field of operations. Nor does the organisation have the resources to handle tourism issues.

Despite this, they do contribute expertise if someone in the tourist industry comes to them for help:

> *"We focus specifically on the industry and making sure that we service our client and primarily we do that with a direct relationship with packages, location packages. We also obviously work with them from community affairs perspective, but not in terms of the film tourism aspect. Our focus is on the production industry, tourism is more outside our [business]... We work as functional expertise if the tourism side comes to us/.../but we do not have the resources to be able to commit to that and it is really outside our mandate because we are specific to production and location."*

Private land next to the location and setting for the house belonging to the Twilight characters the Swan family. The property owner is making a clear statement that he wants the tourists to keep away from his property.

They describe their work with film tourism as reactive rather than proactive:

> "Tourism British Columbia, that's their mandate to work with travel media and media relations, but we will often, when its film specific, so people are writing an article about Twilight and they want to know, we provide them with information and who to talk to and things like that. But we are more reactive in that side, we are not proactive, mostly because we are a small office and we are busy trying to facilitate direct production activity."

A representative from Tourism Vancouver Visitor Center backs up British Columbia Film Commission's reasoning and says that they also regard their work with film tourism as reactive rather than proactive:

> "[We don't] really market it, so it is more when people show up and we try to help them when they show up, we are mostly reactive when people coming looking for film sets and things 'cause after the film sets aren't published, no one is told where they are 'cause the stars don't wanna be bugged, they wanna get the shooting done."

The representative from the British Columbia Film Commission believes that Tourism Vancouver and the Visitor Center can contribute more when it comes to marketing film tourism in the region:

> "One thing we want to see the Visitor Information Center to do is, for example, have movie posters and posts that are about films in British Columbia, and information about it, what places/locations, et cetera."

Another representative from Tourism Vancouver points out how hard it is to be involved in the early stages of a film production to be able to use it for tourism purposes. Instead, they try to take advantage of the benefits of a film production when the recording has finished and is ready for release in the cinemas. However, it is usually at the next stage, when the film is released on DVD or Blue Ray, that they have the opportunity to get involved. One example of Tourism Vancouver's collaboration with the film industry was a competition with Canada's tourism commission and a travel company in the UK.

The competition was held when one of the Twilight films was released on DVD, which resulted in publicity for Vancouver on the Internet and via thousands of international travel agencies and tour companies. It is estimated that this type of marketing activity can continue for the next five to six years, according to the representative from Tourism Vancouver. He points out that the connection between Vancouver and Twilight has been made clear to Twilight fans, which this competition contributed to:

> *"to the average person living in the United Kingdom who is being approached by this, they probably had no idea the connection between Vancouver and Twilight. So a matter of fact, there are probably thousands of pla-*

ces that they are thinking of going to but the fact that they are Twilight fans number one, someone put us up on a 'higher' position."

A great deal of destination marketing is about creating an image. This means that when an 'external' player, such as the film industry, contributes to creating a particular image for a place (place marketing), this also influences the tourists' experience, the effect of this will be unplanned and surprising if a relationship is not formed at an early stage between the film company and the destination's stakeholders.[47] One of the representatives of Tourism Vancouver describes how in China, which is a new market for Vancouver, not much is known about Canada, but a surprising amount is known about Vancouver. The explanation for this is that Vancouver features in a soap opera that is broadcast in China:

> "So we go to shows and talking to clients who doesn't know about the Rocky Mountains, but they know about Vancouver because they remember seeing us featured in that soap opera-series/.../So that's an example how anything else what you say about Vancouver [is] going to be colored in their eyes by what they saw in that series – for good or for bad/.../Sometimes we also have to be cautious when we get involved with filming, how we want to be positioned."

The British Columbia Film Commission has a large digital library with all the locations that they offer. These are used when they put together presentations for the places/environment that they send to their clients in the film industry. A representative of the organisation emphasises that British Columbia is not British Columbia in the films, but that the region often represents the US. The variety of settings that the region has to offer is highlighted as one of the region's strengths:

"We got desert, mountains, urban cities/…/we can be anything pretty much, except for tropical stuff."

Both Tourism Vancouver and the British Columbia Film Commission state that British Columbia and Vancouver are rarely portrayed as themselves in films and television series, which once again ties to the concept of *local dissonance.* This means it is difficult to use these for tourist and business purposes as the visitor is rarely, or never, aware that it is Vancouver being shown on the screen:

> *"It is difficult to be able to use that, to capitalize on that, sometimes conventional filming where people have a very strong connection with the places being featured in the film. That's usually not the case in Vancouver. Americans often get very surprised when they get to know that X-files is filmed in Vancouver, where Vancouver is stand in for an American city/…/it is not like, 'The Girl with the Dragon Tattoo' series, in that that is location based specific. British Colombia is everywhere. Most people do not know that the films were shot here. So it is harder to promote from a film tourism perspective."*

One of the representatives from Tourism Vancouver says that they have not been capable of assuming a more aggressive position when using film productions to market the region:

> *"We haven't been able to have that position, at least not yet. We continue to focus on this as an added proposition to why to come to Vancouver. We cannot use it as a primary focus because people don't get it."*

A related phenomenon that may be significant for a destination's image is the use of celebrities in marketing. They can affect the image that potential visitors have of a destination, which can lead to an increased likelihood that the visitors choose to travel there. Additionally, celebrities' visits to a place can be the subject of media attention, which can also affect a destination's image.[48] In one context, where destinations use film to change or create an image and to increase tourism, celebrities' role in this process should be highlighted. For example, the film's celebrities can be used for direct marketing of tourism to the place, or comprise an important element in how the film is used to create interest in tourism.[49]

One of the representatives from Tourism Vancouver wishes that the film locations could be more open to the public and that it was possible for visitors to see the actors filming scenes. The result of them not being open to the general public is that visitors first know about the filming when it has finished. The Twilight films are used as a good example of this, according to Tourism Vancouver:

> *"Twilight is a good example, people come and recognize those places and want to experience, and they get the sense of, ok we can go to those places, but of course filming is since long, over."*

The British Columbia Film Commission is interested in using famous actors in their work, but also says that this is not easy, partly because the actors have not themselves chosen the location and partly for political reasons:

> *"One of the things that we would like to do for the Film Commission benefits is to get testimonies, but testimonies can often be very difficult because these high profile actors, they shoot up here because the studios decide that this was the best place to be. So they do not necessarily want to go on how wonderful it is in British Columbia because when they go home it puts them in a difficult*

situation. So sometimes they will because they loved it, but the testimonies have to be something they give when we ask for it, again, we have to be sensitive against our client. What benefits tourism, that's not our first priority, our first is to service clients so that they bring projects here".

The tour operator in Vancouver who offers guided film location tours started her company after realising the level of demand for guided Twilight tours in Forks. She knew that there were fans that travelled to Vancouver to see the locations, but she also knew that they didn't have knowledge of where these places are situated. The demand for her product surprised her, and she describes how it varies:

"I thought that it would be a good idea to make a tour with movie locations where they actually filmed New Moon and then I started that in June 2009 and made my own web site, which I'd never done before, so that was a process/…/I was very surprised and happy when I got bookings/…/It goes up and down, like in the summer time it is very busy when they're filming in Vancouver/…/more people want to come to Vancouver during the filming than any other time because they think there is a chance they might see the cast."

Not allowing the company to grow too much has been a strategic decision on her part, as she does not want it to be so big that she needs to worry that her activities will be too visible to the film production company, among others. As a result of this, she has chosen to use a minibus without the company's name on it:

"I don't want it to get too big so that I have to worry about: 'Oh there is the big van from the tour', no I

don't want that/.../Because the people would go: 'Oh she is doing the movie locations' and that is not always a positive thing."

The tour operator in Vancouver takes the fans to locations that become important servicescapes for the Twilight tourists. Because much of the visitor industry has non-physical components, such as service, the visitor also bases his/her assessment on the physical components that can be seen and touched. The visual impressions of the servicescape consist of several factors, such as colour, light, space, functionality, layout and design. All of these contribute to forming an image in the visitor's mind. The visitor's experience is also based on individual susceptibility, expectations, motivations and knowledge of previous experiences.[50] The servicescape thus influences the visitor's experience and, by extension, behaviour. For example, if the visitor is comfortable with the place's physical attributes, this may result in the visitor choosing to stay longer and to return to it.[51]

A forest glade in British Columbia's rainforest is a significant servicescape for visiting fans. One says: "you just think you are in the movie, it's so wild."

Deserted alleyway in central Vancouver, British Columbia, that was used as a location in the third Twilight film, Eclipse, and which is included in an organised and guided Twilight tour.

There are numerous non-organised servicescapes linked to Twilight in British Columbia. These are former locations that do not have any type of adaptation to tourists' needs using physical attributes. Despite this, these environments generate strong feelings among the tourists who visit them. Examples of such environments are a glade in British Columbia's rainforest and a dirty and deserted alleyway in central Vancouver, that produce strong feelings through the tourists' emotional ties to the characters or events in the films. These natural, non-organised servicescapes are enlivened by a guide during a tour, which has an important role in bringing these servicescapes to life.

As previously described, authenticity is important to film tourism experiences.[52] In British Columbia and Vancouver, many of Twilight's locations are on privately-owned land on which the tourist industry cannot control development. Another problem in creating authenticity is that the production company that builds temporary sets then demolishes them, such as the Swan family's house in British Columbia. This means that

Twilight tourists meet barriers and security staff at the set of the Swan family house at the location in British Columbia, Canada.

tourists do not have the opportunity to visit what to them are authentic landmarks or, and previously demonstrated, are met by signs that say "private property, no trespassing".

The tour operator in Vancouver explains her view of the film locations and how so many simple environments, such as a gravel road, can comprise an attraction with high authenticity:

> *"Because the connection with the movie/.../say it is not so much about seeing some structure or building out in the woods, it is more of seeing and making the connection from what they read in the book to actually seeing how it is going to look in the movie and to have that connection and experience, is exciting."*

During her six-hour long tour she guarantees the authenticity of the experience by describing many details of the filming and thus communicating the genuineness of the experience:

*"I tell you how they got the shot, you know the things
they have to do, how it was set up and how it looked
like and all the different departments involved in making this and all the people that it employs and why
Vancouver is Hollywood North".*

Montepulciano, Italy – throne of
the Volturi vampire clan

Like Volterra, Montepulciano is located in Tuscany, Italy, and
has around 14,500 inhabitants. The town is famous for its fine
wines, as well as for its art and architecture. Montepulciano has
retained its mediaeval character with the walls that surround
the town and it has many well-preserved monuments, a mediaeval square and a well-visited cathedral.[53] Montepulciano is
about a two-hour drive from Volterra.[54] The town has, apart
from the Twilight film *New Moon*, been used as a location for
a number of popular films, including *Under the Tuscan Sun*
(2003), *A Midsummer Night's Dream* (1999) and *The English
Patient* (1996).[55]

The town's press office describes their first contact with Twilight and the filming of the second in the series – New Moon. It
was in the winter of 2009 that a group of Americans visited the
town and requested a tour, with the aim of looking for a location for an unnamed film project. When it became clear that
the film was part of the Twilight phenomenon and that Montepulciano had been chosen as a location, the press officer realised that this decision would change Montepulciano's future:

"I discovered that this movie would change the history in
Montepulciano/.../From that moment on, we had the
craziest period of our history."

The first Twilight tourists arrived in Montepulciano in April
2009, after a journalist found out that the film was going to
be located in the city and spread the news on the Internet. Fil-

ming stopped at the end of May that year, but a lot happened in Montepulciano in the intervening period. The press officer talks about *the crazy week,* as the filming was called locally. During that week the city was full of tourists, including screaming fans, and the little town had around 10,000 visitors every day. This meant that the town's capacity, in terms of accommodation and restaurants, was not sufficient. Montepulciano has estimated that the economic effect of that week was around €2.5 million.

As has been said, the local population's attitude to tourism is an important part of the impression that the visitor gets of the place. Greater pressure on a place's infrastructure could lead to a negative attitude among local residents.[56] The head of business and tourism in Montepulciano believes that New Moon's filming has been very important to all the town's inhabitants, but that there are individuals who object to the resulting tourism:

> "Of course there is always one who is not perfectly in accordance now with the mass, but, it was the case of just one shop because he had problems to find parking, but nothing else."

The town's press officer also describes his experience of how Twilight tourists blocked the entrance to a public building during the busy summer months:

> "We don't want to wait to enter inside the City Hall because it never happened before, but in the summer for example it was really difficult to enter the City Hall/.../ to go to work, because of the people taking the pictures, and this is very strange and funny because in Montepulciano we don't want to wait for something like that."

The opportunity to market a destination in association with a film is created both when the film has its premiere and later when it is released on different markets at different times and in other formats (e.g. DVD and Blue-Ray).[57] The press officer in Montepulciano calls this *The DVD Effect*:

> *"Because who came in town after they saw the movie in the cinema was a certain part, but then when [the] movie was published all over the world [on DVD], the number of tourists increased."*

As regards the authenticity of the Twilight experience, the press officer doesn't see any major problem in the town being a location, while the nearby town of Volterra is where the events are set:

> *"We actually didn't suffer about this, maybe the Volterrian suffer about the decision to set the movie in Montepulciano and not in their town. We think that is enough for us that when the people in the cinema watch the movie and [Twilight-character] Alice landed in Italy and said to Bella 'here we are in Volterra', a lot of people in the cinema, more than hundred people screamed something like 'this is not Volterra, this is Montepulciano'. We think that this is enough for us/.../ of course in Volterra they are quite luckier than us, because they started to be part of this movement, Twilighter movement, because of the book/.../so even before the movie everyone knows about what happened in Italy."*

A Twilight tourist guide in Montepulciano also shares Volterra's opinion that the Twilight tourists travel to both Montepulciano and Volterra during their Twilight experience in Italy:

"Of course here we have Twilighters coming here because they want to see the places where it was set. In Volterra there are the readers of the book, but concerning my personal opinion in guiding people even for the New Moon tour, generally big fans do both/.../first they visit Volterra because they are a fan of the book, and then they visit Montepulciano because they are a fan of the movie."

The head of business and tourism in Montepulciano points out another perspective relating to authenticity, when he highlights the importance of balancing the town's history with new Twilight tourism:

"We can thank everyone for choosing the town, but we don't want to be considered the city of the vampires, we want to be Montepulciano, the town where the New Moon movie was set also/.../we would like to underline that we are in Montepulciano and not in the vampire town."

What both these Italian Twilight destinations have in common is that they want to preserve their history and identity, and choose to strategically include these in the Twilight experiences for visiting fans. One example that the Twilight guide in Montepulciano describes is how, during the Italian school holidays, many children visit the town and are also told about the town's history and heritage during the New Moon guided tour:

"As a tourist guide, I can say that this was the only occasion on which I saw with my eyes a teenager looking at me/.../following my explanation about the history of the town/.../they ask a lot of questions, interested, because generally you talk about Montepulciano and maybe there are also nice stories, funny stories, happening in town about the Middle Ages, but no one is in-

terested in them/.../but [it's] not [like that] with New Moon."

As with Volterra, Montepulciano has no organised servicescapes for Twilight tourists. Despite this, the town's square and city hall with its clock tower (which was apparently why Chris Weitz – the Twilight film's director – chose to locate filming in the town), are the most significant servicescapes for the fans; ones where they, time and again, recreate scenes from the film. The most photographed servicescape is the steps and entrance to the city hall's clock tower:

> *"Everyone who comes to the town, and even if they don't have a tour, they have their special pictures in front of the square, and they all were in the same position in which Robert Pattinson came out from/.../the doorway of the city hall."*

As previously described, guided tours and maps of locations are important tools in creating this form of tourist experience.

Souvenir shop with Twilight products in Montepulciano, Italy.

As with a number of other Twilight destinations (Forks, Volterra), it was the town's tourist office that was responsible for the initial development of Twilight tourism and these tools. In addition to the tourist office's work, a significant element in product development was a local shop owner's purchase of the copyright for the use of New Moon in marketing the town and its products. In addition to the shop owner's own production of items such as T-shirts, vampire capes and vampire wine, he also donated the rights to the municipality, which is now responsible for using them. The press officer for the town believes that the products that have been developed are successful:

> *"We didn't make something special, we just bought the copyright because it is impossible to use the name 'New Moon', and that's it, but we can say that the t-shirts, the bags, so all stuff connected to the fans, that have been having a good market, so great number of pieces were sold during the season/…/even the tours that we propose to the Twilighters, they are working well".*

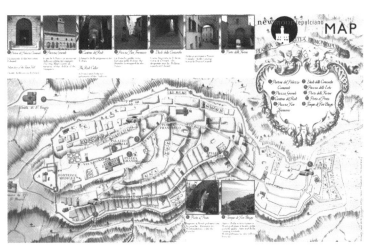

Montepulciano's New Moon map with marked locations from the film. Published with the permission of the tourist office in Montepulciano.

126

References

[1] **Frost**, W. (2006) Braveheart-ed Ned Kelly: Historic Films, Heritage Tourism and Destination Image. *Tourism Management, 27*(2), 247–254.

Frost, W. (2006) *From Backlot to Runaway Production: Exploring Location and Authenticity in Film-Induced Tourism.* Working Paper Series ISSN 1327-5216 presented at Second International Tourism and Media Conference in Melbourne, Monash University, Department of Management, Australia.

Frost, W. (2009) From Backlot to Runaway Production: Exploring Location and Authenticity in Film-Induced Tourism. *Tourism Review International, 13*(2), 85–92.

[2] **Murphy**, P., Pritchard, M.P. & Smith, B. (2000) The Destination Product and Its Impact on Traveler Perceptions. *Tourism Management, 21*, 43–52.

[3] **Murphy**, P., Pritchard, M.P. & Smith, B. (2000) The Destination Product and Its Impact on Traveler Perceptions. *Tourism Management, 21*, 43–52.

[4] **http://www.forkswashington.org**/police-chief [Retrieved: 7th of October 2011]

[5] **http://en.wikipedia.org**/wiki/Forks,_Washington [Retrieved: 25th of August 2011]

[6] **http://en.wikipedia.org**/wiki/Quileute_people [Retrieved: 26th of November 2011]

[7] **http://en.wikipedia.org**/wiki/Quileute_people) & http://www.quileutes.com/breaking-dawn/quileutelegends.html [Retrieved: 26th of September 2011]

[8] **http://www.quileutenation.org**/ [Retrieved: 26th of November 2011]

[9] **Palmer**, A. & Bejou, D. (1995) Tourism Destination Marketing Alliances. *Annals of Tourism Research, 22*, 616–629.

[10] **Murphy**, P., Pritchard, M.P. & Smith, B. (2000) The Destination Product and Its Impact on Traveler Perceptions. *Tourism Management, 21*, 43–52.

[11] **Murphy**, P., Pritchard, M.P. & Smith, B. (2000) The Destination Product and Its Impact on Traveler Perceptions. *Tourism Management, 21*, 43–52.

[12] **Sautter**, E. & Leisen, B. (1998) Managing Stakeholders: A Tourism Planning Model. *Annals of Tourism Research, 26*, 312–328.

[13] **Sautter**, E. & Leisen, B. (1998) Managing Stakeholders A Tourism Planning Model. *Annals of Tourism Research, 26*, 312–328.

[14] **Sheehan**, L. & Ritchie, J.R (2004) Destination Stakeholders Exploring Identity and Salience. *Annals of Tourism Research, 32*, 711–734.

Currie, R.R., Seaton, S. & Wesley, F. (2008) Determining Stakeholders for Feasibility Analysis. *Annals of Tourism Research, 36*, 41–63.

Freeman, R. (1984) *Strategic Management: A Stakeholder Approach.* Pitman: Boston.

Palmer, A. & Bejou, D. (1995) Tourism Destination Marketing Alliances. *Annals of Tourism Research, 22*, 616–629.

Sautter, E. & Leisen, B. (1998) Managing Stakeholders: A Tourism Planning Model. *Annals of Tourism Research, 26*, 312–328.

Tkaczynski, A., Rundle-Thiele, S.R. & Beaumont, N. (2009) Segmentation: a Tourism Stakeholder View. *Tourism Management, 30*, 169–175.

[15] **Sheehan**, L. & Ritchie, J.R (2004) Destination Stakeholders Exploring Identity and Salience. *Annals of Tourism Research, 32*, 711–734.

[16] **http://www.twilightlexicon.com/**2009/06/02/quileute-nation-hires-pr-professional/[Retrieved: 28th of September 2011]

[17] **http://www.twilightlexicon.com/**2009/06/02/quileute-nation-hires-pr-professional/[Retrieved: 28th of September 2011]

[18] **Beeton**, S. (2006) Understanding Film-induced Tourism. *Tourism Analysis, 11*(3), 181–188.

[19] **Palmer**, A. & Bejou, D. (1995) Tourism Destination Marketing Alliances. *Annals of Tourism Research, 22*, 616–629.

[20] **Hudson**, S. & Ritchie, J.R. (2006) Film Tourism and Destination Marketing: The Case of Captain Corelli's Mandolin. *Journal of Vacation Marketing, 12*(3), 256–268.

[21] **Bitner**, M.J (1992) Servicescapes: The Impact of Physical Surroundings on Customers and Employees. *Journal of Marketing, 56*, 57–71.

Lin, I. Y. (2004) Evaluating a Servicescape: The Effect of Cognition and Emotion. *International Journal of Hospitality Management, 23*, 163–178.

Lam, I. Long, W. Ka Wai, C. Davis, F. Freda, L. (2011) Does the Look Matter? The Impact of Casino Servicescape on Gaming Customer Satisfaction, Intention to Revisit, and Desire to Stay, *International Journal of Hospitality Management, 30*, 558–567.

Lin, I.Y. (2012) Servicescape Moderation on Personality, Traits, Emotions, Satisfaction, and Behaviors. *International Journal of Hospitality Management, 31*, 31–42.

Mossberg, L. (2007). A Marketing Approach to the Tourist Experience. *Scandinavian Journal of Hospitality and Tourism, 7*(1), 59–74.

[22] **Lin**, I. Y. (2004) Evaluating a Servicescape: The Effect of Cognition and Emotion. *International Journal of Hospitality Management, 23*, 163–178.

Shiffman, L.G. & Kanuk, L.L. (1978) *Consumer Behaviour*. Prentice-Hall: Englewood Cliffs, NJ.

[23] **Lam,** I. Long, W. Ka Wai, C. Davis, F. Freda, L. (2011) Does the Look Matter? The Impact of Casino Servicescape on Gaming Customer Satisfaction, Intention to Revisit, and Desire to Stay, *International Journal of Hospitality Management, 30,* 558–567.

[24] **Murphy**, P., Pritchard, M.P. & Smith, B. (2000) The Destination Product and Its Impact on Traveler Perceptions. *Tourism Management, 21,* 43–52.

[25] **http://www.stepheniemeyer.com**/twilight.html [Retrieved: 3rd of October 2011]

[26] **MacCannell**, D. (1973) Staged Authenticity: Arrangements of Social Space in Tourist Settings. *American Sociological Review, 79,* 589–603.

[27] **Knudsen**, Timm, B. & Waade, A.M. (2010) *Re-Investing Authenticity: Tourism, Place and Emotions.* Short Run Press Ltd: Bristol.
MacCannell, D. (1973) Staged Authenticity: Arrangements of Social Space in Tourist Settings. *American Sociological Review, 79,* 589–603.
Buchmann, A., Moore, K. & Fischer, D. (2010) Experiencing Film Tourism: Authenticity & Fellowship. *Annals of Tourism Research, 37,* 229–248.

[28] **Buchmann**, A., Moore, K. & Fischer, D. (2010) Experiencing Film Tourism: Authenticity & Fellowship. *Annals of Tourism Research, 37,* 229–248.
Wang, N. (1998) Rethinking Authenticity in Tourism Experience. *Annals of Tourism Research, 26,* 349–370.

[29] **Frost**, W. (2006) Braveheart-ed Ned Kelly: Historic Films, Heritage Tourism and Destination Image. *Tourism Management, 27*(2), 247–254.
Frost, W. (2006) *From Backlot to Runaway Production: Exploring Location and Authenticity in Film-Induced Tourism.* Working Paper Series ISSN 1327-5216 presented at Second International Tourism and Media Conference in Melbourne, Monash University, Department of Management, Australia.

[30] **Buchmann**, A., Moore, K. & Fischer, D. (2010) Experiencing Film Tourism: Authenticity & Fellowship. *Annals of Tourism Research, 37,* 229–248.
Knudsen, Timm, B. & Waade, A.M. (2010) *Re-Investing Authenticity: Tourism, Place and Emotions.* Bristol: Short Run Press Ltd.

[31] **Hudson**, S. & Ritchie, J.R.B. (2006) Film Tourism and Destination Marketing: The Case of Captain Corelli's Mandolin. *Journal of Vacation Marketing, 12*(3), 256–268.
Hudson, S. & Ritchie, B. (2006) Promoting Destinations via Film Tourism: An

Empirical Identification of Supporting Marketing Initiatives. *Journal of Travel Research*, *44*, 387–396.

[32] **Frost**, W. (2006) *From Backlot to Runaway Production: Exploring Location and Authenticity in Film-Induced Tourism.* Working Paper Series ISSN 1327-5216 presented at Second International Tourism and Media Conference in Melbourne, Monash University, Department of Management, Australia.

[33] **http://en.wikipedia.org**/wiki/Quileute_people [Retrieved: 26th of September 2011]
http://www.quileutes.com/breaking-dawn/quileutelegends.html   [Retrieved: 26th of September 2011]

[34] **http://www.ne.se/volterra** [Retrieved 24th of August 2011]
http://www.volterra.se/sevardheter/ [Retrieved 24th of August 2011]

[35] **Frost**, W. (2006) *From Backlot to Runaway Production: Exploring Location and Authenticity in Film-Induced Tourism.* Working Paper Series ISSN 1327-5216 presented at Second International Tourism and Media Conference in Melbourne, Monash University, Department of Management, Australia.

[36] **Palmer**, A. & Bejou, D. (1995) Tourism Destination Marketing Alliances. *Annals of Tourism Research, 22*, 616–629.

[37] **Palmer**, A. & Bejou, D. (1995) Tourism Destination Marketing Alliances. *Annals of Tourism Research, 22*, 616–629.

[38] **Collins**, T. & Doorley, T. (1991) *Teaming up for the 1990s: A Guide to International Joint Ventures and Strategic Alliances.* Homewood: Irwin.
Palmer, A. & Bejou, D. (1995) Tourism Destination Marketing Alliances. *Annals of Tourism Research, 22*, 616–629.

[39] **Palmer**, A. & Bejou, D. (1995) Tourism Destination Marketing Alliances. *Annals of Tourism Research, 22*, 616–629.

[40] **Hudson**, S. & Ritchie, J.R.B. (2006) Film Tourism and Destination Marketing: The Case of Captain Corelli's Mandolin. *Journal of Vacation Marketing, 12*(3), 256–268.

[41] **Murphy**, P., Pritchard, M.P. & Smith, B. (2000) The Destination Product and Its Impact on Traveler Perceptions. *Tourism Management, 21*, 43–52.

[42] **http://www.ne.se**/lang/british-columbian [Retrieved:11th of October 2011]

[43] **http://en.wikipedia.org**/wiki/Hollywood_North [Retrieved:11th of October 2011]

[44] **Croy**, W.G & Walker, R.D. (2003) Fictional Media, Film and Tourism. In D.

Hall, L. Roberts & M. Mitchell [Eds], *New Directions in Rural Tourism*. Asshgate: Aldershot UK, 115–133.

Frost, W. (2006) *From Backlot to Runaway Production: Exploring Location and Authenticity in Film-Induced Tourism.* Working Paper Series ISSN 1327-5216 presented at Second International Tourism and Media Conference in Melbourne, Monash University, Department of Management, Australia.

[45] **Frost**, W. (2006) *From Backlot to Runaway Production: Exploring Location and Authenticity in Film-Induced Tourism.* Working Paper Series ISSN 1327-5216 presented at Second International Tourism and Media Conference in Melbourne, Monash University, Department of Management, Australia.

[46] **Hudson**, S. & Ritchie, J.R. (2006) Film Tourism and Destination Marketing: The Case of Captain Corelli's Mandolin. *Journal of Vacation Marketing, 12*(3), 256–268.

[47] **Connell**, J. (2005) Toddlers, Tourism and Tobermory: Destination Marketing Issues and Television-Induced Tourism. *Tourism Management, 26*(5), 763–776.
Hudson, S. & Ritchie, J.R. (2006) Film Tourism and Destination Marketing: The Case of Captain Corelli's Mandolin. *Journal of Vacation Marketing, 12*(3), 256–268.
Hudson, S. & Ritchie, J.R.B. (2006) Promoting Destinations via Film Tourism: An Empirical Identification of Supporting Marketing Initiatives. *Journal of Travel Research, 44*(4), 387–396.

[48] **Glover**, P. (2009) Celebrity Endorsement in Tourism Advertising: Effects on Destination Image. *Journal of Hospitality and Tourism Management, 16*(1), 16–23.

[49] **Young**, A.F. & Young, R. (2008) Measuring the Effects of Film and Television on Tourism to Screen Locations: A Theoretical and Empirical Perspective. *Journal of Travel & Tourism Marketing, 24*(2), 195–212.

[50] **Lin**, I.Y. (2004) Evaluating a Servicescape: The Effect of Cognition and Emotion. *International Journal of Hospitality Management, 23*, 163–178.
Shiffman, L.G. & Kanuk, L.L. (1978) *Consumer Behaviour*. Prentice-Hall, Englewood Cliffs, NJ.

[51] **Bitner**, M.J (1992) Servicescapes: The Impact of Physical Surroundings on Customers and Employees. *Journal of Marketing, 56*, 57–71.
Lin, I.Y. (2004) Evaluating a Servicescape: The Effect of Cognition and Emotion. *International Journal of Hospitality Management, 23*, 163–178.
Lam, I. Long, W. Ka Wai, C. Davis, F. Freda, L. (2011) Does the Look Matter? The Impact of Casino Servicescape on Gaming Customer Satisfaction, Intention to Revisit, and Desire to Stay, *International Journal of Hospitality Management, 30*, 558–567.

Lin, I.Y. (2012) Servicescape Moderation on Personality, Traits, Emotions, Satisfaction, and Behaviors. *International Journal of Hospitality Management, 31*, 31–42.

[52] **Buchmann**, A., Moore, K. & Fischer, D. (2010) Experiencing Film Tourism: Authenticity & Fellowship. *Annals of Tourism Research, 37*, 229–248.

Knudsen, Timm, B. & Waade, A.M. (2010) *Re-Investing Authenticity: Tourism, Place and Emotions.* Short Run Press Ltd: Bristol.

[53]   **http://www.consorziovinonobile.it**/107–46/ITA/MONTEPULCIANO-EIL- SUO-TERRITORIO [Retrieved: 9th of September 2011]

http://www.turismo.intoscana.it/intoscana2/export/TurismoRTen/sito   TurismoRTen/Contenuti/Itinerari/visualizza_asset.html_135228851.html   [Retrieved: 1st of October 2011]

http://www.montepulciano.net/ [Retrieved: 35th of September 2011]

http://www.nautilusmp.com/tuscany/presentazione/montepulciano/indexing.html [Retrieved: 35th of September 2011]

[54] **http://maps.google.se/** [Retrieved: 11th of October 2011]

[55] **Thesan & Turan** (2009) *Montepulciano Film Commission.*

[56] **Palmer**, A. & Bejou, D. (1995) Tourism Destination Marketing Alliances. *Annals of Tourism Research, 22*, 616–629.

[57] **Hudson**, S. & Ritchie, J.R.B. (2006) Promoting Destinations via Film Tourism: An Empirical Identification of Supporting Marketing Initiatives. *Journal of Travel Research, 44*(4), 387–396

Measuring and evaluating the effects of pop culture tourism

"It has touched all types of businesses. Even if it is not Twilight related and lodging. We have more choices as residents. More shopping, more things to do. Forks Coffee Shop was planned to close, but so did the tourists start coming …and other examples to. It is pretty hard to define, we haven't had so many new business recently but there have been some, we have a new bakery just open, we had taxi, so they are not too Twilight but obviously dependent of it. So the effects are far reaching! I do not think that you can't find a business in town that hasn't benefited hugely from it!"

Manager at the visitor center in Forks, Washington,
on the Twilight effect

Research literature contains no established and accepted method for measuring the marketing value of a film in relation to a destination. The difficulties in measuring the effects of both the marketing value and the multiplier effect[1] of a film being located in a region are highlighted by a representative of the British Columbia Film Commission:

"it is difficult from a data capture prospection to properly measure the economic impact of this industry because it has a spill over effect on so many broad base industry sectors. A significant amount is spent in goods and services"

---

[1] The money that is spent and invested in a region during a film production, which creates growth in several areas.

However, within tourism research, there are studies that illuminate the value of marketing for tourism and within media research, there are methods for measuring the value of the publicity for a particular media phenomenon.[1] Calculations have been made on the basis of the increased tourism to a place after filming, based on the level of increase in tourism (overall tourism statistics) in relation to the level of tourism before filming (and the film premiere). Additionally, a more long-term effect can be measured, in that increased tourism from one market may increase interest in buying property in the area and thus making the effects of film tourism more permanent, as there is growth in the number of returning tourists.[2] The equivalent addition of tourism to a place has been documented by Connell, who also demonstrates that an entirely new target group was attracted to the destination. In Connell's study, the positive effect of increased tourism was mainly experienced by hotels and restaurants.[3] The staff at the tourist office in Forks describe a similar effect in their town:

> *"Motels were very interested to getting people out here because Forks has always been kind of thought of: too far to go there. **But now we are not**."*

A calculation of the marketing value linked to the *Lord of the Rings* films has been conducted by the New Zealand Institute of Economic Research.[4] The calculation is based on the size of the audience and a number of other assumptions (compared to traditional marketing arenas) which, translated as commercial value, was the equivalent of almost USD 42 million. One study of the effects of film tourism in New Mexico, USA, estimated the annual income to be 1,450 jobs and USD 168 million, distributed as tourists' spending and state and local taxes, for example.[5]

A method called Monetary Publicity Value (MPV) is used for evaluating a destination's image based on a publicity value, and was introduced by Castelltort and Mäder. The method uses the cost of what the equivalent area of an editorial text would be, based on the cost of advertising in the same media. The higher the MPV, the higher the publicity efficiency. The method is often used in the PR industry. MPV should be regarded as an approximate value of the marketing effect of media space. The process for measuring the value is: collection of media material, systematisation of subjects/areas, selection of media material for analysis, systematisation of sources, evaluation of selected material in terms of effect on various target groups (should be based on validated studies of target group behaviour) and calculation of MPV. The result of an MPV analysis can be used by a destination to evaluate strengths and weaknesses in its profile, for example. MPV is a relatively simple method that takes account of the effect on various target groups, because the advertising cost is placed in relation to the size of each media's target group, and the size of the media space. The method can also be used for media other than printed media, where there is an advertising cost. The weakness of the method is primarily that the value is an indication of a potential effect, but not a value for an actual effect.[6]

A form of MPV was used in the evaluation of the Swedish Millennium films' effects on the Stockholm region. Marketing value is called exposure value in the evaluation, which is based on the equivalent method for calculating product placement. This is based on how many times Stockholm is publicised (with tourist image associations) per film and the audience size of each film. This value is compared to the equivalent value for traditional advertising time. They have also added the exposure value of media reporting and advertising.

The same evaluation also estimated the business film tourism that occurs as a result of a film being located in a region and the resulting multiplier effect. The Millennium films' production budget was around SEK 100 million, of which SEK 93 million was spent or invested in the region (e.g. through services, accommodation, transport, wages). The multiplier effect was estimated to be 1.5 (a figure based on previous multiplier effects in similar cases), which generated a socio-economic value that was equivalent to SEK 140 million.[7]

In socio-economic assessments of film production, traditional factors such as employment, accommodation, transport/infrastructure, facilities investments and other expenditure in the form of other consumption, catering and peripheral services are included.[8] The socio-economic value of filming (using examples such as *Varg [Wolf]* and *The American*) has also been assessed in a study in Jämtland, Sweden, where multiplier effects were estimated at 5.4, which generated an effect of SEK 2.7 million in the case of the film *Varg*. The socio-economic value was based on a ratio of the money invested by the region and the amount the film production company spent in the region during filming.[9]

In summary, it can be stated that many of the measuring instruments for both marketing value/exposure value of film, film tourism's other effects and multiplier values for filming that are currently used have weaknesses. However, there is a great demand for measurement models to measure the effects, both from the film production side and from regions that are affected by filming and what it can provide in terms of jobs, infrastructure and tourism. This is summarised by a representative of the British Columbia Film Commission in Vancouver:

"it will definitely be beneficial if we could come up with a reliable way to measure the industry outside what we do and that is production's expenditure"

Another criticism of existing measurement models is that they are unable to include soft factors[10], such as an increased sense of pride and belonging in the local population and the film as a bearer of local heritage. The mayor of Forks describes how the Twilight books and films convey the local Quileute people's heritage, which he sees as a positive effect from Twilight:

> *"I think one of the lasting things out of this too will be a greater appreciation for the North West native cultures, that's something that's going to last for decades."*

The negative effects of this form of tourism, such as limitations in the local carrying capacity for managing large numbers of new tourists[11], are rarely included in the measurement models described above. Nor are negative effects such as increased prices, image distortion of the place in the film, or the result of visitors searching for untraditional souvenirs in the form of public property, such as road signs[12], usually included in these measuring instruments for social benefit.

Twilight's long-term effect on the destinations is believed to be – by all of the smaller Twilight destinations (Forks, Volterra och Montepulciano) – that Twilight has changed their branding forever, regardless of whether Twilight tourists will continue to travel to these destination in the future or not. The press officer and head of trade and industry in Montepulciano summarise this in the following manner:

> *"[It] was so important because Montepulciano now is well-known around the world, and this is just because of the movie. Then, the reason for which the tourists continue to come here is just for the movie, or just for the wine, or just for the art; the important [thing] is that they discover Montepulciano/.../It's impossible for... Montepulciano to have so much money to spend in commercialising the image of Montepulciano, so that was for free."*

The Twilight Tours. One of the Twilight tour operators in Forks, WA, USA.

The mayor of Forks is of the same opinion, and believes that Twilight has put their little town on the map for many fans around the world, who will return for reasons other than Twilight in the future:

> "We generally talk about people coming here for Twilight with a good experience and just a warm feeling, loving the scenery, loving the area and coming back years in the future with the families, so I think we look at it like families coming back for the rest of their lives, will it be Twilight related? Probably not, I mean, fads come and go, so at some point we have to be really, I think as a community to kind of just let it go and remember it for what it was".

References

[1] **Kulendran**, N. & Divisekera, S. (2007) Measuring the Economic Impact of Australian Tourism Marketing Expenditure, *Tourism Economics, 13*(2), 261–274.

[2] **Hudson**, S. & Ritchie, J.R.B. (2006) Promoting Destinations via Film Tourism: An Empirical Identification of Supporting Marketing Initiatives. *Journal of Travel Research, 44*(4), 387–396.

[3] **Connell**, J. (2005) Toddlers, Tourism and Tobermory: Destination Marketing Issues and Television-Induced Tourism. *Tourism Management, 26*(5), 763–776.

[4] **NFO New Zealand** (2003) *Lord of the Rings Market Research Summary Report*, Wellington: NFO New Zealand.

[5] **Southwest Planning & Marketing and CRC & Associates** (2008) *The Impact of Film Tourism in the State of New Mexico*, Report for New Mexico Tourism Department. [http://www.denniskintigh.com/tourism.pdf Retrieved: 9th of October 2011].

[6] **Castelltort**, M. & Mäder, G. (2010) Press Media Coverage Effects on Destinations – A Monetary Public Value (MPV) Analysis. *Tourism Management, 31*(6), 724–738.

[7] **Cloudberry Communications** (2011) *Milleniumrapporten: Ekonomiska effekter av Stockholmregionen i de svenska Millenniumfilmerna.* Report for Filmregion Stockholm-Mälardalen, Regionförbundet Sörmland, Film i Sörmland and Stockholm Business Region Development.

[8] **Johnsson**, A. & Pettersson, R. (2006) *Effekter av en regional filmproduktion – med utgångspunkt från en Jämt-Tröndersk filmkommission.* Utredningsserien U2006:30, ETOUR, Mid Sweden University.

[9] **Lundström**, C. (2011) *I spåren av Clooney och Stormare: Kan film skapa regional utveckling och turism?* Report for Mid Nordic Filmcommission 2008–2011.

[10] **Johnsson**, A. & Pettersson, R. (2006) *Effekter av en regional filmproduktion – med utgångspunkt från en Jämt-Tröndersk filmkommission.* Utredningsserien U2006:30, ETOUR, Mid Sweden University.

[11] **Tooke**, N. & Baker, M. (1996) Seeing is Believing: The Effect of Film on Visitor Numbers to Screened Locations. *Tourism Management, 17*(2), 87–94.

[12] **Riley**, R., Baker, D. & Van Doren, C.S. (1998) Movie Induced Tourism. *Annals of Tourism Research, 25*(4), 919–935.

Twilight tourism in transition

In the light of development and events related to the Twilight Saga phenomena between October 2011 and August 2012, this chapter has been added compared to the Swedish edition of the book. The purpose of this chapter is hence to give the reader an idea about the current status of pop culture tourism related to the Twilight Saga.

"This too shall pass"
Middle-Eastern proverb[1]

One of the biggest challenges for a potential pop culture tourism destination is to decide whether to invest in this form of tourism and, if so, to what extent. Important questions include: *How long will it last? Will there be a return on investment?* All tourist destinations undergo different stages of development and pop culture tourism destinations are no exception. On the contrary, since these destinations are founded on pop culture phenomena that are transitory in nature, they are perhaps more subject to changes than others.

One of the most referenced and widely used models of destination development stages, or a destination life cycle curve, is Butler's[2] (1980) Tourism Area Life Cycle (TALC model). It consists of seven different phases: exploration, involvement, development, consolidation, stagnation, decline and rejuvenation. During the *exploration stage* a small number of tourists visit the destination, primarily made up of early explorers of a particular form of attraction/destination. At this stage, the interaction between these visitors and local residents is likely to be high, with no specific facilities provided for visitors.

During the *involvement stage,* visitor number starts to increase and, as a result, some locals will start to get involved in providing facilities for tourists. In the development of this stage, target groups of visitors and tourist season(s) may emerge. Furthermore, initial efforts to develop tourism will be made by government and public agencies. In the *development stage,* there is a larger influx of tourism facilities provided by external organizations and there will be noticeable changes to the physical environment. As the season peaks, it is not uncommon for there to be a larger number of tourists than the permanent local population.

During the *consolidation stage,* the rate of increase in visitor numbers will decline, though the numbers are still increasing. A significant proportion of the destination's economy will be based on tourism and some opposition against tourism can be found among its residents. The next stage – *stagnation* – is characterized by visitor numbers that have reached a peak. Furthermore, the destination will have a well-known image, but the destination and its product are no longer fashionable. Some destinations may experience that capacity levels have been reached or exceeded.

For some destinations, the *decline stage* comes next. At this stage, the destination can no longer maintain its position vis-à-vis newer destinations and attractions. As a result, some tourist facilities are closed down, in line with decreasing demand. Some destinations are able to move on to a *rejuvenation stage,* during which many attractions are changed to attract new tou-

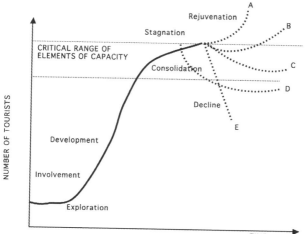

Figure 1. The Tourism Area Life Cycle (Butler, 1980).

rists. For some destinations, this entails building new man-made attractions or utilizing previously untapped natural resources to build new attractions. In order for rejuvenation to take effect, both private and government investments are necessary.[3]

In order to address the concerns that some potential pop culture tourism destinations may have about investments, we will discuss the development of Twilight tourism destinations over time. In 2012, Twilight tourism at all of the destinations had reached a stagnation or rejuvenation/decline phase. In the US for example, Twilight tourism in Forks, Washington, has remained fairly steady over time. However, over the last couple of years the number of tourists has stagnated or declined following the all-time high in 2010. However, it is notable that the number of visitors is substantially higher than prior to the Twilight era and they still receive visitors from all over the world as a result of Twilight.[4] Bill and Susan Brager, proprietors of Miller Tree Inn B&B, also known as "Cullen House", describe the latest development in Forks' Twilight tourism:

> *"For us, though Twilight has certainly passed its peak, it is still very important to our business. For a small 8 room B&B having even 1 guest because of Twilight that would not otherwise have come, is a big deal."*[5]

Marcia Bingham, Director of Forks' Chamber of Commerce, summarises the development of Twilight tourism over the last couple of years and the decline in visitor numbers:

> *"Nonetheless, we are still a "hot topic" and visitors who come once are likely to return. We've heard many times, "we came for <u>Twilight</u>: we'll be back for Forks." This is a quote we relish! Our visitor numbers are still higher than they ever were prior to the books and movies being released, and we have name identification internationally that we didn't have before."*[6]

Year	Number of visitors
2005	5575
2006	6386
2007	10,295
2008	18,736
2009	69,675
2010	72,885
2011	45,579

Table 1. Visitor numbers at Forks' visitor center, Washington, US.

Bill and Susan Brager continue to describe the Forks visitor numbers in the following way:

> "2010 was our best year ever in regard to the number of tourists. We had our best occupancy figures in our 14 years as innkeepers. We noticed a slight increase in occupancy in 2008, more in 2009 and then it peaked in 2010. 2011 was a good year, better than 2009, but not as good as 2010. So far, 2012 has been around 10% off from 2011. In April we saw our biggest decrease of about 21%. Our May looks pretty good and we think our summer will be good. There is a bit of a spike in activity around the release of the movies, but it is fairly short lived."[7]

Forks has also noticed a change in the demographics of its guests. This change consists of less teenagers and more women aged 20 plus. "Girls' weekend away" get-togethers are more popular than mother/daughter/grandmother/granddaughter or teenage girl birthday parties.[8]

A much sharper downturn of numbers of Twilight tours can be seen in Vancouver, Canada. One tour operator reports that the demand for her tours has decreased to a third of the previous year. Two explanations are provided for this sudden decrease in demand: firstly fans appear to have moved on from Twilight and secondly, the production company behind the Twilight Saga has forced the tour operator not to market her products:

> *"the production people were very aggressive in shutting me down all together, there wasn't an opportunity to advertise or promote my Tours as Twilight Tours on the internet or anywhere else."*[9]

Cara Vanderhall at Vancouver's tourist office states that they have not witnessed much of a change as regards Twilight tourism at the destination during the last year. Her experience is that most of the momentum regarding Twilight tourism was during filming and that after it ended, interest from fans has declined.[10]

At the Twilight destination of Montepulciano, Italy, they have also experienced a decline in demand for their Twilight tours. However, the interest in the town as a result of being featured in the second Twilight movie New Moon has not decreased from either foreign or domestic visitors; Twilight tourists in Montepulciano are still teenagers who are travelling with their parents, as well as more mature fans between 27 and 40 years of age.[11]

New strategies and product development have been implemented as a result of the changes that have taken place at the Twilight destinations. In Forks, for example, the Forks Chamber of Commerce is promoting not only "Twilight", but also a number of outdoor activities that visitors can participate in, such as kayaking, hiking, rafting, surfing, fishing, and a new adventure activity called zorbing[1], all utilising the destination's

---

[1] Zorbing is the recreation or sport of rolling downhill in an orb, usually made of transparent plastic.

natural resources. One of the town's disappointments was the closing down of Dazzled by Twilight souvenir shop, and another store has scaled back its Twilight section. The latter has moved into selling "Forks" items, rather than strictly Twilight products, which are available from online retailers. A few other stores and restaurants have also closed down, but this could be a result of the nation's weakened economy rather than being related to Twilight tourism.[12] Marcia Bingham at Forks' tourist office describes the situation as follows:

> *"Economically, Forks is in a challenging condition currently but we are confident we will climb out of it and continue to be a destination for fans of the books and movies/.../we are confident we will remain on peoples' bucket lists of places they want to visit".*[13]

A number of other organisational changes have been implemented in order to attempt to rejuvenate the destination. For example, there are new organisers for the Stephenie Meyer Day that was previously orchestrated by the Chamber of Commerce. This re-organisation has resulted in a number of new product ideas, including plans to open a Twilight museum. Furthermore, the Chamber of Commerce is implementing new campaigns in order to compensate for the decreasing media attention and the free advertising the destination previously received due to its association with Twilight.[14] Also, on a micro level, there is evidence of an optimistic outlook on Twilight tourism at the destination. One example is the Three Rivers Resort, which is also known as the "Treaty Line" between Forks and La Push, where investments have been made in brand new Twilight signs and an expansion of their restaurant.[15]

In Vancouver, Canada, a Twilight tour operator explains that she has now moved on to primarily offering other tours than Twilight, such as film location fan tours which include visiting popular film and television series locations around

Greater Vancouver, as well as wine tours in British Columbia.[16] Vancouver Visitor Centre does not expect any changes to Twilight tourism, as Vancouver is often used as a stand-in for other cities in feature films and series:

> *"Many of the filming locations in our area are inaccessible or not recognizable so many fans won't see what they saw in the movies when they arrive. Vancouver is a very popular location for movies and TV to be filmed, due to the proximity to Los Angeles and the existing talent in the city."*[17]

In Montepulciano, Italy, the city continues to promote itself as it did before Twilight, with the knowledge that Twilight has brought a new tourist segment of young visitors. Twilight merchandise is still available in stores and some vendors use Twilight and New Moon as a way of attracting attention from visitors. When asked about the future of Twilight tourism at their destination, Montepulciano officials state that they expect this form of tourism to slowly decrease, but that the destination will always be associated with the Twilight Saga. They speak from experience, as the destination has previously been featured in hit films such as *The Gladiator* and *The English Patient*.[18]

At the destination which has undergone the most dramatic tourism development in the world because of Twilight – Forks – officials are carefully optimistic about their destination. They expect that the current declining trend in Twilight tourism will continue, with similar numbers of visitors. One explanation is that the final instalment of the film series will be released late in 2012, and other new pop culture phenomenon are starting to capture fans' imaginations.[19] However, new experiences such as Twilight-themed weddings are offered and a permanent servicescape in the form of a Twilight museum is in the making, in order to continue to capitalise on the phenomenon.[20]

In the light of the stagnation, decline or need for rejuvenation in Twilight tourism at established Twilight destinations around the world, it may come as a surprise that new Twilight destinations and tourist experiences are appearing or are increasing. For example, as a result of the fourth movie in the series, there is now a new luxury Twilight destination. In Brazil, where Twilight characters Edward Cullen and Bella Swan spend their honeymoon (and the film is shot), fans can travel to the island of Paraty, take guided tours of locations and stay at the honeymoon six-bedroom house for approximately $4,000 per night.[21]

There is also a continuous flow of Twilight events (official and unofficial) being organised all over the world. Some events are so called procons, which means that they are organised by a professional event organiser. Examples of these are TwiCon or promotion events that are supported by the production or distribution company.[22]

Twilight Saga fan event in Stockholm, Sweden.

In addition to this, there is evidence of a growing number of fancons, which are events organised by fans themselves. Some of these are small in terms of event participants, such as privately organised events to celebrate a DVD/BlueRay release of a Twilight movie or a trip to a Twilight destination organised by a blog user. However, some of these fancons attract larger numbers of visitors, such as the TwiFicMeetUp in Las Vegas in June 2012, when Twilight fanfiction writers and fanfiction fans met to discuss and enjoy one of their favourite pastimes – fanfiction.[23] The explanation for this phenomenon may be found in the transition of these events, from being solely focused on Twilight to fandom-created motives for participating at events such as fanfiction, charity, or to enjoy the fellowship and friendship of other fans.

So, will the fans remain loyal to Twilight? This is not an easy question to answer. Some important characteristics of fans include their involvement, enthusiasm, and emotional attachment. Twilight Saga fans are also known for their openness, creativity, and commitment. Our web survey[24] showed that the level of involvement for Twilight fans has remained high since 2010, even though the peak for general interest in Twilight seems to have occurred in 2010/2011. Asking fans about their future involvement shows that they feel it is very likely that their interest will remain strong, at least until the end of 2012 when also the final film is released. The majority of fans also state that their interest in Twilight has grown since 2010. Fans are still particularly involved through the use of the Internet and communion through social media. These platforms are therefore likely to be important in the transition of Twilight fans even after the final film is released, and will continue to be an important way for fans to stay attached to the fan community and find mutual interests. Furthermore, fans still state that their involvement with Twilight includes purchasing Twilight related products as a reward for themselves or as a way of expressing personality and identity.

What about the transition of Twilight destinations? Based on our research, these destinations can currently best be described as being in the stagnation or rejuvenation/decline phase of the tourism area life cycle. That implies that they are all challenged by the need for innovation. In tourism, market demand is an important driving force.[25] In the case of Forks, market demand for Twilight tourism has been created by so called "lead-users" or "first-movers", who had a need prior to others finding it. Forks has now grown as a tourist destination in parallel with the growth of market demand. However, it is critical that the destination is able to integrate the tourists with the innovation process in order to find the next innovation, one which will either let Forks remain at a high level in terms of the number of Twilight tourists, or to begin another tourism destination life cycle with a new offer that suits market demand. Integrating the tourists is important, because they are the real experts on their individual needs; tourists are never only passive recipients of tourism experiences, since they actually co-create experiences with other tourists and with tourism businesses. Still, tapping into the tacit knowledge that tourists possess about their needs and experiences may not be an easy thing, but the first step is to acknowledge tourists as a source of valuable knowledge. Additionally, forming relationships with the many creative and committed online communities that are associated with travel and tourism in general, and with Twilight in particular, can be of use when looking for market demand.

From the perspective of a destination's resources, it is also important to note that many types of innovation may be necessary for long-term development and success. For example, niche innovations[26] can include inviting new categories of companies, such as businesses in other sectors of the creative industry, foreign investors, or suppliers of other complementary products, into the tourist sector. Also, creating marketing alliances, new combinations of existing products and activating small-scale tourism resources, for example those with links to local society and culture, are all examples of strategies for niche innovation. Another example of type of innovation that may follow is a more architectural type of innovation. [27] This means using new types of resources in the creation of tourism products, for instance, or redefining the use of certain areas for tourism.

References

1 **http://en.wikipedia.org/wiki/This_too_shall_pass**

2 **Butler**, R.W. (1980). The Concept of a Tourist Area Cycle of Evolution: Implications for Management of Resourses. *The Canadian Geographer,* 24(1), 5–12.

3 **Butler,** R.W. (2006). *The Tourism Area Life Cycle Vol 1: Applications and Modifications.* Aspects of Tourism, Channel View Publications: Clevedon, UK.

4 **Email** correspondence with Mike Gurling and Marcia Bingham, Forks Visitor Center, May 2012.

5 **Email** correspondence with Bill and Susan Brager, Miller Tree Inn B&B aka Cullen House in Forks, WA, US, May 2012.

6 **Email** correspondence with Marcia Bingham, Forks Visitor Center, May 2012.

7 **Email** correspondence with Bill and Susan Brager, Miller Tree Inn B&B aka Cullen House in Forks, WA, US, May 2012.

8 **Email** correspondence with Mike Gurling and Marcia Bingham, Forks Visitor Center, May 2012.

9 **Email** correspondence with location tour operator in Vancouver, Canada, May 2012.

10 **Email** correspondence with Cara Vanderhall, Vancouver Visitor Center, May 2012.

11 **Email** correspondence with Francesca Raspanti, Strada del Vino Nobile di Montepulciano, May 2012.

12 **Email** correspondence with Marcia Bingham, Forks Visitor Center, May 2012. **Email** correspondence with Bill and Susan Brager, Miller Tree Inn B&B aka Cullen House in Forks, WA, US, May 2012.

13 **Email** correspondence with Marcia Bingham, Forks Visitor Center, May 2012.

14 **Email** correspondence with Bill and Susan Brager, Miller Tree Inn B&B aka Cullen House in Forks, WA, US, May 2012.

15 **Email** correspondence with Mike Gurling, Forks Visitor Center, May 2012.

16 **Email** correspondence with location tour operator in Vancouver, Canada, May 2012.

17 **Email** correspondence with Cara Vanderhall, Vancouver Visitor Center, May 2012.

[18] **Email** correspondence with Francesca Raspanti, Strada del Vino Nobile di Montepulciano, May 2012.

[19] **Email** correspondence with Mike Gurling, Forks Visitor Center, May 2012.
Email correspondence with Bill and Susan Brager, Miller Tree Inn B&B aka Cullen House in Forks, WA, US, May 2012.

[20] **www.twilightweddingsinforks.com** [Retrieved: 3rd of July 2012]

[21] **www.newworldreview.com**/2012/02/rent-brazils-twilight-house-its-in-paraty/ [Retrieved: 3rd of July 2012]

[22] **www.twilightconvention.com**/cal/twilight_il.htm [Retrieved: 3rd of July 2012]

[23] **www.twificmeetup.blogspot.se/** [Retrieved: 3rd of July 2012]

[24] **International web survey** on "Twilight, tourism and social media" ETOUR Mid Sweden University. Contact: Christine Lundberg (Christine.Lundberg@miun.se)

[25] **Buhalis**, D. (2000). The Tourism Phenomenon: The New Tourist and Consumer. In C. Wahab, & C. Cooper (Eds.), *Tourism in the Age of Globalization*, (pp. 69–96). Routledge: NY.

Hall, C. M, & Williams, A.M. (2008). *Tourism and Innovation*. Routledge: London.

[26] **Abernathy**, W. J., & Clark, K. B. (1985). Innovation: Mapping the Winds of Creative Destruction. *Research Policy*, *14*, 3–22.

[27] **Abernathy**, W. J., & Clark, K. B. (1985). Innovation: Mapping the Winds of Creative Destruction. *Research Policy*, *14*, 3–22.

The unknown future of pop culture tourism

Pop culture tourism's sustainability and future

Perhaps the most frequent criticism aimed at pop culture tourism is whether it is sustainable in the long term. To what extent should destinations dare to invest in a tourist attraction that is based on something as transient as a pop culture phenomenon? Previous studies on such phenomena have shown that *direct effects,* in the form of increased travel flows to a destination that result from filming in the region, for example, can be expected to decline after around four years. However, these studies do not include the sometimes extensive, *indirect* effects of the same phenomenon. Such effects may be people choosing one destination over another because of its association with a film, television series or book. This is particularly interesting because pop culture is consumed by many people around the world, some of whom will take decisions to travel based upon the impression they have received. The fact that a destination has been portrayed through pop cultural forms of expression, such as films, books or music, so arriving on the consumer's 'mental map' can, in turn, result in the marketing that is communicated about the destination being noticed more by the potential tourist. In this way, this form of marketing can also mean that the tourist chooses one destination rather than another.

The marketing effect that occurs due to a destination being portrayed in film or literature is almost incontestable, but the results of this can be both positive *and* negative. Examples of documented positive effects are an increased number of visitors to the destination, broadened target groups (new pop culture tourists that supplement existing tourist groups), changed image and extended seasons. However, the exposure of a destination through forms of expression associated with pop culture can also lead to negative effects, such as the crowding out of existing target groups, attracting the wrong target groups, loading on existing infrastructure and the local carrying capacity for hosting visitors, as well as a damaged destination brand and local identity. The effects are thus not only of a financial nature, despite this being the focus of many existing measurement models in film tourism.

The difficulties of measuring the effects, along with the nature of pop culture tourism – that it is so strongly demand driven and it occurs suddenly – mean that this form of tourism is difficult to plan for. Accordingly, it requires a great deal from the destination, as regards finding a balance between exploitation when the opportunity arises for short-term profit and strategic work to achieve long-term positive effects for the destination. Additionally, it places demands on the destination's ability to develop parallel images of the destination; they must attract the new pop culture target group, but also live up to the existing target group's needs, motivations and expectations. Those destinations that monitor pop culture phenomena that may be relevant to their destination have an advantage over the destinations that are suddenly overwhelmed by pop culture tourists and which thus need to work reactively simply to manage a sudden demand, rather than planning for it strategically. Our hope is therefore that destinations will collect information from other industries in the future, such as the creative industries, when formulating tourism strategies. In this way, new opportunities and demands from closely related industries can be discovered and strategically developed for the destination, as well as preventing negative effects such as image problems and stresses on local carrying capacity (for example, infrastructure).

What is necessary for a destination to succeed with pop culture tourism? Research has proposed a number of success factors for film tourism, grouped in several categories. The first deals with different types of destination attributes, such as landscape, available filming sites, sets and icons. The other relates to film specific factors such as the film's success, identifiable and accessible places, the film's history in relation to the place, the amount of exposure on the screen and an attractive image. However, before the film is made, a number of other factors are necessary for film tourism to result from it. These are investments from the state and film commissioner in the form of lobbying, tax relief, dedicated websites, location scouting services and public relations. Others cover place-specific resources such as infrastructure (for example, studios, physical accessibility), labour and local expertise. Some of these are also relevant to other forms of pop culture tourism, while some are more specific to film tourism. In general, it is important to identify future pop culture tourists through a deepened understanding of the fans of various phenomena, whether they be music, literature, film/TV or something else.

Tourism and pop culture
– a meeting of two industries

One of the biggest challenges facing the tourism industry when investing in pop culture tourism is building a relationship and cooperation with the creative industries. As this book's content demonstrates, these two industries use different logic. One example that illustrates this is the view of information and its dissemination. The tourism industry builds upon the dissemination of information about destinations, attractions and offers to large target groups, while the film industry's logic builds upon limiting the spread of information about filming and locations during pre-production and filming. Additionally, the potential tourist attractions, such as former filming sites, are often private and public areas with limited opportunities for adaptation for tourism once production is over. A vital element of cooperation between the industries is the negotiation for the use of copyright materials by the tourism industry in their future exploitation for tourism purposes. Our hope is that the destinations that are active in acquiring knowledge of pop culture phenomena and trends, ones that may affect their destinations, are also active at an early stage in initiating partnerships with the relevant production companies or publishers. This may involve a municipality actively investing in a film production that is going to be located in its administrative/geographic area. Such investment may even entail securing usufruct to utilise film locations or brands in future marketing and tourism materials.

Up to the present day, there are few examples of clear strategic cooperation between the creative industries and tourism. The focus has been on the tourism income that film, for example, generates in the region in direct income and multiplier effects during production. Our opinion is that the creative industries have a lot to gain from interest in their products having a long life and being reinforced, disseminated globally, creating varied forms of customer value and receiving greater exposure, such as through tourism. That people who are interested in a particular film, television series, book or type of music also travel to places associated with the phenomena should strengthen their ties to it, and also spread that interest to others over a longer period of time. Travelling is a way for fans to express their interest in a pop culture phenomenon whilst also buying the books, music, watching the film at the cinema and/ or buying it for private use at home, spreading information and knowledge of it to others via word of mouth. The latter is regarded as a very important source of information, both within tourism and creative industries.

Places, storytelling and authenticity

The importance of pop culture tourists being able to visit places that are linked to their interest is well documented. This form of travel has been described as a modern form of pilgrimage in which the tourist walks in his/her favourite character's footsteps, sees what the character saw, does what the character did and feels what the character felt at that specific place. You can say the tourist carries strong feelings linked to the characters, people or events at the place visited and thereby creates his/her own experience. In some cases, pop culture travel is also about the feeling of getting really close to a character or celebrity, for example, an actor or musician, by visiting a place with which that person is associated.

The environments, or servicescapes, that are visited by pop culture tourists may either be adapted to the visitors (for example, with signs, themed products and souvenirs) or non-adapted (places that are completely without adaptation to the visitor). Thanks to the tourist carrying his/her own emotional link to the place through his/her relationship with a favourite character, person or event, even a non-adapted environment can create strong positive experiences and satisfaction. Storytelling is a significant tool in these experiences. It is used via different forms of themed products through which a story is told, but also via personal guides, who use their stories to create authentic experiences. The major challenge as regards pop culture sites is how to use them while maintaining them for tourism purposes. This could be using sets left after filming, or agreements with private individuals and authorities for the use of environments that are private or public property. It is also about finding a balance between exploiting a place for the purposes of pop culture tourism and retaining the place's authenticity, such as the local history and identity.

Fans, fellowship and the media

Tourism is a global industry with great potential for growth and strong competition. This poses a challenge to individual stakeholders in finding unique offers for target groups with changing needs. Pop culture and fans comprise a specific form of tourism and a target group that builds on people's deep involvement with various films/shows, books, sport or music. For many fans, this involvement means that it permeates several aspects of their lives, such as fashion, their own creativity, education and travel. Besides this, it is often an involvement that remains for a long time, making them a type of loyal customer who is happy to spread their interest to others. These are important qualities for the development of tourism.

Tourism is driven by people's needs and wishes to move themselves from a place in everyday life to something more desirable. They are attracted by the different aspects of a destination that they experience as being able to fulfil these needs and wishes. This is in clear agreement with what being a fan entails; people are attracted by a pop culture phenomenon because it is the opposite of their everyday life. Research shows that fans who are also tourists are driven by motives that are more generally applicable to travel, such as escape from everyday life, entertainment and socialising with others. However, fans are also driven by psychological and sociocultural motives that are more emotionally charged, such as aesthetic pleasure, drama, interaction with icons and symbols, fellowship in a group with shared norms, routines, rituals and language. This social fellowship is of extra importance and makes it possible to share downs and ups with others, thereby gaining satisfaction.

Apart from fans having close links between the perception they have of themselves and the phenomenon in which they are interested, social identity in relation to other people is also important. Groups of fans create common meaning for each other; networks, both online and offline, make it possible for them to exchange experiences and information and to create joint interpretations of their interest, or even jointly create books and films (fan-fiction).

Pop culture tourism is now growing on the basis of the growth of the creative industries and the information society that makes it possible to spread information and communicate with others in simple and effective ways. The media's increased significance for how people create images of places, for example, is also an important aspect of the growth of pop culture tourism. The Internet is particularly increasing in importance as a source of information and as a communication channel;

fans can easily fulfil their need for information and contact with other fans through using the various social media and networks. Social media are interactive, dynamic and participant-focused. They are also functional, social and exploratory, making it possible to build relationships, learn new things, be creative and escape from everyday life. This means that social media and networks are well suited to the needs and motivations that fans express. For example, our research shows that Twilight fans make extensive use of the Internet when planning trips and sharing their experiences, and that this is an important channel for them in developing and shaping their involvement. It is clear that it is on the web that pop culture tourism's development will be decided. This is where information is spread and interpreted at the speed of light. This is where reasons to travel and the necessary information for travel planning are disseminated, relationships and networks are formed and comprise potential future visitors to various destinations; this is where destinations' images are formed or entirely new destinations are discovered! The fans' use of the Internet in general and social media in particular is thus a driving force for innovation in both the creative industries and in tourism.

In summary, we believe pop culture tourism will grow in the future. Fandoms and new technology, as well as creative tourist destinations, are central to this and success will depend on the courage of entrepreneurs, the fans' commitment and involvement, online creativity, knowledgeable stakeholders, both public and private, and capital and investments. From a research perspective, we look forward to opportunities for gaining knowledge about these complex but fascinating questions in the future.